Meeting the Guidance and Counseling Needs of Boys

Lawrence Beymer, PhD
Indiana State University

AMERICAN
COUNSELING
ASSOCIATION

5999 Stevenson Avenue
Alexandria, VA 22304

Meeting the Guidance and Counseling Needs of Boys

10 9 8 7 6 5 4 3 2 1

American Counseling Association
5999 Stevenson Avenue
Alexandria, VA 22304

Director of Communications
Jennifer L. Sacks

Acquisitions and Development Editor
Carolyn Baker

Production/Design Manager
Michael Comlish

Copyeditor
Heather Jefferson

Cover design by Martha Woolsey

Cover photo © 1990 Tom McKitterick, Impact Visuals

Library of Congress Cataloging-in-Publication Data

Beymer, Lawrence.
    Meeting the guidance and counseling needs of boys/Lawrence Beymer.
        p.   cm.
    Includes bibliographical references.
    ISBN 1-55620-136-2
    1. Teenage boys—Counseling of. 2. Young men—Counseling of. I. Title.
HV1423.B49   1995
362.7'0835'1—dc20   94-31000
                                                                                              CIP

TABLE OF CONTENTS

ABOUT THE AUTHOR

Lawrence Beymer is chairperson of the Indiana State University Department of Counseling. A former school counselor, his graduate degrees are from Purdue and Michigan State Universities.

His research and teaching concentration has been on techniques and supervision of counseling and career and life planning. Recently, he headed a 3-year, state-wide gender equity project involving 71 middle and junior high schools. He is a recipient of the Indiana Counseling Association's "Counselor Educator of the Year" award.

Currently, Dr. Beymer is involved as a guidance consultant to 10 professional development schools in a multi-year school renewal project funded by the Lilly Endowment. He is also a participant in Project UNITE—a coalition of nine national universities working for the improvement of those who teach urban children in poverty.

He and his wife, Norma, a school counselor, are parents of one son and three daughters.

PREFACE

For many centuries, being young has been perceived by adults as a time of joyful existence. The preacher in Ecclesiastes wrote the following many centuries ago: "Rejoice, O young man, in thy youth; and let thy heart cheer thee in the days of thy youth, and walk in the ways of thine heart, and in the sight of thine eyes" (chap. 11, verse 9).

Many boys today would respond, "That's easy for him to say." The fact is, it has never been easy to be a boy or to make the transition to manhood. Evidence abounds that many boys today are not mastering either as well as both they and society would prefer; and to make matters worse, the challenges are not getting any easier.

The purpose of this book is to draw the attention of counselors and other youth workers to some selected aspects of life that are challenging boys today, and to make some constructive suggestions for professional guidance and counseling services that have the potential of improving the results for everybody involved.

PATTERNS OF INDIVIDUAL AND GROUP DIFFERENCES

Much of this book draws on accumulated literature that more often than not consists of research investigations. Therefore, a review of some of the basic procedures and assumptions of measurement seems warranted.

Measurement is the assignment of numbers to observations according to certain conventions and rules. Such information can be used to describe the status of an individual or a group, or to make comparisons between groups, or both.

Differences Between Individuals

One of the basic and most universally acknowledged findings of psychology research is the confirmation of the existence of individual differences. Like snowflakes, each human being has an exclusive and unique design. A stroll along any beach in July confirms that we differ physically. However, abstract psychological differences are not as easy to detect and quantify.

Differences Within and Between Groups

When the same data are collected from large numbers of individuals, a range of findings usually results. The initial or raw data must be summarized using the techniques of descriptive statistics to increase their meaning. Usually this begins with the calculation of a measure of central tendency, usually the average (mean), and a measure of variability, usually the standard deviation.

The means and standard deviations of any two comparison groups are seldom identical; that would be truly astonishing. The question always arises as to *why* they are different: whether the differences observed are real, or merely the result of accident and chance, traceable to imprecision in the measuring process. This question is answered using the techniques of inferential statistics.

Meaningful and Meaningless Differences

Much confusion is caused by the dual definitions of the word *significant*. In everyday use, we tend to use this word to refer to something that is meaningful, important, and worthy of notice. Statisticians, however, use the word *significant* to refer to findings that are not likely traceable to chance factors. In other words, a significant difference between two groups is one that is not likely due to chance errors of measurement.

The problem is that the difference between two groups can be statistically significant, but meaningfully insignificant to practitioners. For example, a midwestern state recently spent millions of dollars to reduce school class sizes by a few pupils. Evaluation results showed less than a single point improvement for the smaller classes over the larger class control group. That tiny difference was statistically significant, but represented insufficient justification for the expenditure required to produce it. A statistically significant difference may have irrelevant implications for practitioners.

Group Confidence, Individual Uncertainty

Another complication in interpreting differences is related to the fact that studies provide us with information about groups, whereas we as counselors deal with individuals. Norm-based predictions are very accurate, and can forecast with considerable precision. Unfortunately (or fortunately), they cannot indicate whether the client across the desk conforms to the prediction. The fact that 60% of boys who made a certain aptitude test score did not go on to pass the math course may be absolutely true from past experiences, but the counselor never knows for certain what the current odds are, or if the client earning that same score today will pass or fail the course.

Differences Between the Sexes

When conducting studies, it has always been easy and convenient to note, record, and analyze the age and sex of participants. Both are examples of objective information that can easily be used to divide the sample for data comparisons. A mountain of descriptive data has been collected over the years about males and females. Sex of subjects is an obvious, permanent, and relevant condition that is easy to note when collecting data. Sifting and summarizing research evidence has produced statements of central tendency and variability that are presented throughout this book.

Throughout the volume, references are made to how young males' conditions, characteristics, and status differ from those of young females. Neither as individuals nor as sex groups are we created equal, despite considerable poetic pretense to the contrary. However, opinions differ among reasonable people on how such differences are best explained. Which are inherent to the sex and must be acknowledged and accepted, and which are the consequences of arbitrary practices that can be altered by those who are in the business of fostering healthy growth and development?

GENERALIZATIONS, SIMPLIFICATIONS, AND STEREOTYPES

Communicators often simplify complex issues for clarity and exaggerate them for emphasis. Advertising specialists, politicians, and editorial cartoonists build careers using these techniques. The trick is to seek out, but to stop short of crossing, the boundaries between generalizations and overgeneralizations—between simplifications and oversimplifications.

A *stereotype* is an example of a generalization—a simplification, an exaggeration. Ironic as it may seem, even the stereotype has been stereotyped as something offensive, negative, hostile, and hurtful, and to be avoided. Not all stereotypes are rigid, biased, and without some essence of truth. Counselors use stereotypes constructively every time they interpret the Holland (1985) codes and Myers–Briggs (1962) types. Holland classified everybody into one of six categories: realistic, investigative, artistic, social, enterprising, or conventional. The Myers–Briggs test uses many combinations of generalizations, such as extroversion–introversion, sensing–intuition, thinking–feeling, and judging–perceiving. A generalization based on the best current knowledge is useful in communicating ideas, even if it is labeled a *stereotype*.

There seems little choice but to begin with the best evidence we have about status and differences, and modify and moderate interpretations knowing that individuals can and do vary from general tendencies. Despite all of the complications and reservations listed previously, differences between males and females do exist, and many of them are important and worthy of notice. Why they exist is not of real importance in this book; rather, the illumination of their presence and efforts to find suggestions about what can be done to address them appropriately and professionally are the concerns here. Boys are fundamentally different in ways that must be understood by anyone who wants to be helpful.

Insights on the nature and nurture of young males can come from several sources, including professional graduate study and practical experience. Some counselors (i.e., male counselors) have the additional advantage of having once been boys themselves, although a majority of counselors were not. For counselors of both sexes, it is hoped that this book provides insights and understandings about boys, and offers some constructive suggestions on how the needs of this important segment of our population can be better served.

The following chapters present a review of selected literature and a presentation of selected studies emphasizing general and specific developmental needs of boys.

Chapter 1 surveys biological differences between the sexes. The environment is important, but the biological foundation was there first. Chapter 2 addresses masculinity; maleness is a given, but masculinity must be attained. Chapter 3 discusses young male sexuality—something that occurs earlier, more frequently, and is more complex than most adults seem to acknowledge. Chapter 4 looks at boys in schools—not always a compatible combination. Chapter 5 views boys in the family—a socialization process potentially positive, sometimes negative, but never neutral. Chapter 6 presents material on friends and gangs—one potentially for better, and the other always for worse. Chapter 7 examines boys in the workplace—a role frequently in competition with their role as students. Chapter 8 focuses on career and life planning—a process beneficial for all, but provided well for only a few. Chapter 9 suggests that, although after all is said and done usually more is said than done, it does not have to be that way.

REFERENCES

Holland, J. (1985). *Making vocational choices* (2nd ed.). Englewood Cliffs, NJ: Prentice-Hall.

Myers, I., & Briggs, K. (1962). *The Myers–Briggs type indicator.* Palo Alto, CA: Consulting Psychologists Press.

CHAPTER 1

BIOLOGICAL INFLUENCES
ON BEHAVIOR

Any discussion of meeting a young male's needs must begin with a consideration of inherent biological factors and forces. Biological differences can be identified while the fetus is but a speck of tissue in the mother's womb, and can progress to include a long list of biochemical, genetic, structural, and organ distinctions.

The relative dominance of nature or nurture, of heredity or environment, has been a long-standing debate. Authorities differ on which is most important, but one thing is clear: Biological factors are always present first.

CASTING THE DIE

Mother nature has many patterns and procedures for determining the sex of her various species. In birds, the mother's sex chromosomes determine the sex of the chick; the female simply releases an egg of the desired sex, and the fertilizing sperm has no function in the determination. For turtles, the sex of the hatchling is determined by the temperature at which the egg is incubated: Eggs nested in cool shady places produce males, whereas those incubated in sunny areas develop into females.

For the human species, sex is determined at the moment of conception by the type of sperm from the father that wins the race to the mother's waiting egg. The biological mother's egg always contributes an X chromosome; the biological father's sperm can contribute either an X or a Y chromosome. If one of his sperm carrying an X chromosome merges with the egg, the resulting fetus will be female. If the sperm that merges with the egg is carrying a Y chromosome, the fetus will be male (Doyle, 1989).

Because sperm carrying X and those carrying Y are produced in approximately equal numbers, it would appear that the chances for male or female are 50–50, but the situation is more complicated than that. During and immediately after wars, when husbands return home after long absences, more sons than usual are born (i.e., the "returning soldier effect"). Males in certain occupations produce more daughters than sons, including fighter pilots, abalone divers, and anesthetists. Older fathers are more likely to produce daughters, whereas older mothers are more likely to produce sons. Why these and other patterns exist is not known, but speculations abound (Ridley, 1993).

At conception, male fetuses outnumber females by at least 115 to 100. However, because of the greater likelihood of spontaneous abortion of the male embryo, the sex ratio for live births drops to about 105 males for every 100 females (Reinisch, Gandelman, & Spiegel, 1979). By age 30, the ratios are approximately equal, but from there on females outnumber males. The proportion of males to females begins to decline from that point on, as more males die off in every age category. By age 65, there are only 65 males per 100 females; by age 80, there are only 50 males per 100 females. These ratios are more accurate for the White population; the situation is much more extreme for the African-American population because of higher death rates for young African-American males.

One great disadvantage of XY over XX is less space for genetic material. Not only is there less surface on Y than X, but also the Y chromosome is smaller. The result is less total capacity to carry genetic material. As a consequence, it is impossible for all recessive genes from the mother's X chromosome to be overcome by a dominant gene from the father (Doyle, 1989).

This is one explanation for why males suffer from a long list of sex-linked biological problems and deficiencies. Montagu (1953) listed over 30 serious disorders that occur in much greater frequency among males, including color blindness, glaucoma, hemophilia, and muscular dystrophy.

Early in the pregnancy, male and female fetuses possess identical external sexual structures. Sometime in the third month of pregnancy, a gene on the Y chromosome causes the male embryo's sex gland to develop into testes, which produce the powerful hormone testosterone. Development of external and internal male organs then accelerates (Groves & Schlesinger, 1979). The testosterone level remains relatively high for 3 or 4 months after birth, then diminishes for the next 10 to 12 years until the onset of puberty (Doyle, 1989). The consequences of emerging sexual male adolescent awareness and expression is discussed in a later chapter.

The geneticist Dr. Anne Moir gathered and organized a wealth of research to demonstrate how male and female brains differ dramatically in chemistry, structure, organization, and internal operation. She concluded that because the sexes differ so much biologically, the fact that they behave differently is inevitable, predictable, and probably unchangeable by sociopolitical pressures (Moir & Jessel, 1991).

DIFFERENCES GOOD AND BAD

The following generalizations about the biological characteristics of males must be taken into consideration when attempting to understand and deal with their behavior. As usual, all generalizations are in comparison to females.

1. The life span of males is, on the average, more than 7 years shorter.
2. Males are more likely to suffer asthma, allergies, ulcers, hernias, baldness, myopia, color blindness, dyslexia, hemophilia, glaucoma, back problems, and attention deficit-hyperactivity disorders.
3. Males have worse senses of taste and smell, are more sensitive to light, are less sensitive to loud sounds, and tend to favor the right ear when listening.
4. Males operate at higher levels of blood pressure, and their blood clots faster. Their testosterone triggers production of a substance that clogs their less pliable blood vessels, resulting in a much higher rate of coronary heart disease.
5. Males are taller, stronger, have less body fat, more upper body strength, more muscle fibers, and are more likely to be left-handed.
6. Growth changes at puberty are seldom smooth and orderly. Extremities grow first, resulting in hands, feet, noses, and ears outdistancing surrounding structures. When bones lengthen before muscles, temporary awkwardness and clumsiness often result.

7. Structural differences in brain tissue have been discovered, although exact meanings and implications are debatable. The outer cortex of the male brain tends to be thicker, and the bundle of nerve fibers that connects the right and left hemispheres of the brain tends to be smaller.
8. The brain is affected by the male hormone testosterone. Males display more physical aggression in public, at least through adolescence. Boys are more active, boisterous, and rough-and-tumble.

Other sex differences related to academic activities are presented and discussed in a later chapter.

AN EXTREME PERSPECTIVE

One school of thought contends that all social behavior has a biological basis. Sociobiology proponents contend that observed behavior is rooted in the genes and developed and expressed for biological reasons (Wilson, 1975). For example, DeVore (cited in Staff, 1977) suggested that what we call *masculine behavior* is little more than a strategy to attract and impress females. "Males," he stated, "are a vast breeding experiment run by females." In other words, each sex controls the behavior of the other by either responding to or ignoring the signals emitted. If females select older mates because they are more likely to control resources, then males find younger females more receptive. If females respond to acts of machismo and bravado, then males will learn to display them.

Sociobiology seems to have a biological interpretation for almost all behavior, from aggression to altruism. Therefore, to some extent sociobiology can be as threatening as psychoanalysis; many find the claims of psychodynamics on the dominating influence of unconscious motivation fascinating, but also threatening. Most of us would prefer to believe that we are rational creatures who choose to act in certain ways—that we are not destined to do things because we must. In a similar fashion, there is considerable resistance in the absence of conclusive data that so much of behavior can be explained by biological adaptions. Although the evidence produced thus far on sociobiology is controversial and inconclusive, it is a point of view worth noting when considering the biology of boys.

IMPLICATIONS FOR COUNSELORS

Many counselors were trained to be facilitators of problem solving. They were taught that there is a solution to every presented situation, and that working together, client and counselor can find and implement it to solve the problem. What is sought is the "wise decision" or the "best answer."

Problems have solutions. For example, the boy who finds that an academic load of chemistry, physics, calculus, advanced composition, and band, in addition to varsity football and a part-time job, is resulting in lowered performance in all areas has a problem. An answer can be formulated that will ease the situation.

More often than not, clients present situations for which there are no solutions. What is needed is to devise a set of behaviors that makes it possible to manage a situation that is at least temporarily immune from substantial solution. This is the difference between a problem and a predicament. Health problems like diabetes and myopia are predicaments: The individual has to learn how to live with them by modifications in diet, medication, and eye glasses or contacts.

Anything undergoing remodeling and transformation can be in a temporary mess. The definition of an *adolescent* as "an adult under construction" is an apt one; it is the basis for many situations that parents and educators often term as *problems*, but that are in fact more accurately conceptualized as developmental predicaments to be managed and tolerated until self-correcting forces restore balances. One rule of thumb is that if a situation is typical for a boy at his particular stage of development, it is more likely to be a predicament than a problem. Although the difference may be subtle, it is important in goal setting to understand the difference between finding an answer versus finding a way to manage and control the inevitable.

The boy who is suffering shame and ridicule because of delayed puberty can be conceptualized as dealing with a predicament—a situation that must be managed, a situation that cannot be "solved" by anything he or he and his counselor can do directly about the situation until the male hormones have their effect. For many boys, not being an athlete and not being perceived by your peers as being athletic is a handicap in early and middle growing-up stages. Many adult men can vividly recall the humiliation they felt decades ago on the playground: by being the only player left for the last side to choose, by dropping a fly ball, or by watching games from the bench. These can be permanent wounds similar to those of young women who, even at middle age, wince when they remember how difficult it was when their physical maturity occurred earlier or later than their peers, or the time they had no date for the prom.

Although biological factors are often beyond direct modification, counselors can be more effective by taking into consideration the biology of boys. Consider the following possibilities.

It is important that young boys learn what is normal in male development, both physically and psychologically. Something is tagged as *abnormal* when and if it differs so much from what is expected that it bothers the observer. Thus, an event can move from *abnormal* to *normal* by an enlightened understanding of the situation. No later than the middle school years, boys should be taught what lies just ahead as they begin the journey from preadolescence to and through adolescence. Before situations become critical and charged with emotion, they can understand what to expect and how to respond appropriately.

Ways must be found to recognize the reality and meaning of *differential maturity*. Boys do not develop at the same pace and rate. Although we can make confident statements about generalities, the fact is that individual boys of the same chronological age differ in their readiness to profit from information and experiences. Guidance and counseling services must not be one-shot events, but be made available in various forms using various techniques over some period of time. Attention and services must be available when the boy needs them, and that timing may vary.

The "problem or predicament" model is useful, but is further complicated because what is a predicament for one boy could be another boy's problem.

The hormonal tidal wave that sweeps through the adolescent male body also has emotional consequences. Self-consciousness about body image, clumsiness, and voice change can lead to shyness and diminished classroom participation. Sometimes likened to a roller-coaster ride in the dark, young males often express mood changes that are frequently misunderstood by adults. Adults need to be reminded not to take all young male outbursts personally.

Counselors are too few in number and too burdened with a long list of other obligations to assume total responsibility for all developmental guidance services. They can multiply their effect by supporting and encouraging others who devise curricular experiences to incorporate information that facilitates the safe and successful metamorphosis of young boys into young men. It is not the job of the counselor to do it all, but it is the job of the counselor to encourage that it all be done.

In summary, environmental factors and forces are indeed important, but biological factors and forces were in place first, and these form the foundation for future development. Being biologically male is insufficient; one has to come to terms with becoming masculine, and then developing the skills and strategies needed to play all of the other roles and responsibilities expected of the maturing male.

REFERENCES

Dolnick, E. (1993, January 30). In the longevity game, the score is females 6 males 0. *Chicago Tribune*, pp. 1,9.

Doyle, J. A. (1989). *The male experience* (2nd ed.). Dubuque, IA: Wm. C. Brown.

Groves, P., & Schlesinger, K. (1979). *Biological psychology.* Dubuque, IA: Wm. C. Brown.

Moir, A., & Jessel, D. (1991). *Brain sex: The real difference between men and women.* New York: Dell.

Montagu, A. (1953). *The natural superiority of women.* New York: Macmillan.

Reinisch, J., Gandelman, R., & Spiegel, F. (1989). Prenatal influences on cognitive abilities: Data from experimental animals and human genetic and endocrine syndromes. In M.A. Whitting & A.C. Petersen (Eds.), *Sex-related differences in cognitive functioning* (pp. 215–239). New York: Academic Press.

Ridley, M. (1993). A boy or a girl? Is it possible to load the dice? *Smithsonian, 24* (3), 113–123.

Staff. (1977, August 1). Why you do what you do. Sociobiology: A new theory of behavior. *Time,* pp. 54–63.

Wilson, E. O. (1975). *Sociobiology: The new synthesis.* Cambridge, MA: Harvard University Press.

CHAPTER 2

MASCULINITY: CHOOSING AND IMPLEMENTING A ROLE

Male is a status established by biology at the moment of conception. *Masculinity* varies according to whatever a social or cultural group chooses to define as the appropriate appearance and behavior for males in its group. Pittman (1990) suggested that masculinity consists of all those activities and qualities that males think will distinguish them from females, because, "We don't want to be mistaken for girls." These standards, definitions, and codes of conduct vary by culture, social class, race, and religion, and have taken numerous forms throughout history. What remains consistent is that maleness is a given; somehow masculinity must be attained.

POINTS OF VIEW

Masculinity can be and has been conceptualized in several ways.

The Straight-Line Bipolar Scale
This model assumes that pure masculine and feminine points anchor the opposite ends of a straight line, and that any individual can be thought of as occupying some point in between (Doyle, 1989). This model is similar to the 0–14 scale of pH in chemistry, where 0 represents maximum acidic, 14 maximum basic, and the midpoint 7 neutrality— the pH of distilled water.

Many traditional and several modern assessment devices follow this model. For example, in the scoring of the Vocational Preference Inventory (Holland, 1985), six occupations recently occupied by a large majority of males are listed, together with eight recently dominated by a majority of females. If the client marks "yes" for the "male six" and "no" for the "female eight," a maximum "masculine" raw score of 14 is obtained.

This masculinity model has not proved to be very useful. Different tests purporting to quantify the same continuum have produced different results and have low correlations with each other. Using Department of Labor work force sex proportions is circular and subject to change. Occupations that some time ago were occupied by a large majority of one sex are used as indicators of occupational sex type, but today the public sees many female lawyers on television and female pharmacists filling prescriptions. The Department of Labor may conclude that both are male occupations, but the younger generation today may not have this perception. Neither is certain that they perceive entertainers as being feminine, nor experimental laboratory engineers as masculine, although older generations might.

The Multilevel Model
First suggested in the 1940s, this point of view has psychodynamic roots (Doyle, 1989). The assumption is that the personality functions on two levels: (a) conscious and unconscious, and (b) masculine and feminine, making four possible combinations:
1. unconscious and conscious masculinity;
2. unconscious and conscious femininity;
3. unconscious femininity and conscious masculinity; and
4. unconscious masculinity and conscious femininity.
Like so many hypothetical constructs based on psychodynamic ideas, validating this model and using it in assessment is difficult, and it has not gained prominence in practice.

The Three Alternatives Scale
This model assumes that there is a third state of affairs called *androgyny*—a blending of certain arbitrarily desirable masculine and feminine characteristics. The concept of androgyny is derived from Carl Jung's writings (cited in Streiker, 1989). Androgyny is an alternative sex role model that surfaced in the late 1960s; it accelerated in popularity in the 1970s in response to cultural shifts in sex roles and accompanying dissatisfaction with the usefulness of the traditional models (Bem, 1976, 1978). Androgyny is more a model of a New Age goal of what could be than a description of what can be shown to exist by research.

The Pleck Point of View

Pleck (1981) constructed a comprehensive model of masculinity that places more emphasis on society's standards and expectations than innate psychological sources. Pleck suggested that a male's attempts at masculine behavior is his attempt to live up to what he perceives to be society's standards and expectations. Because the perceived standards are often confusing, contradictory, and inconsistent, he finds it almost impossible to conform to all of them simultaneously. Sometimes he finds few opportunities to exhibit those qualities he believes society expects. When he finally discovers that he cannot live up to all of the demands he believes others expect, the result can be loss of self-esteem and a variety of dysfunctional behaviors.

The Pleck social strain theory would seem to explain the behaviors that counselors observe in many young male adolescents today, as the latter struggle to convince themselves and others that they are, indeed, unmistakenly masculine. Pittman (1990) wrote that young adolescent males engage in recklessness, taking risks, showing off for older boys, and "bouncing [our] absurdly puffed-up masculinity off one another" in an attempt to confirm masculinity.

CONTEMPORARY CONCEPTIONS OF MASCULINE BEHAVIOR

When parents first recognize that they are caring for a male infant, they begin a process called "sex role socialization." Every culture seems to have expectations and standards for sex-appropriate behavior. These social expectations are called *sex roles*, and they are well under construction long before the child ever sets foot into a school. Several observers have identified what they believe society expects and demands of any male who wishes to be perceived as being masculine.

Brannon (1976) presented a 4-point guide for behaviors considered masculine:

1. No Sissy Stuff: The boy must reject any and all stereotyped feminine characteristics.
2. The Big Wheel: He must strive for conspicuous success and be admired for it.
3. The Sturdy Oak: He must act tough and be confident and self-reliant.
4. Give 'Em Hell!: He must be aggressive, daring, and violent.

Cicone and Ruble (1978) identified three dimensions of the contemporary stereotypical male:
1. Active and Achievement Oriented: How he handles his life: be active, adventurous, independent, courageous, competitive, and successful.
2. Dominant: How he handles others: be aggressive, dominant, assertive, boastful, and place himself over and against others.
3. Level Headed: How he handles his psyche: be logical, realistic, stable, unemotional, self-controlled, cool, and self-contained.

Doyle (1989) listed five elements in the contemporary North-American conception of the male role:
1. Antifeminine: Reject anything that is identified with females.
2. Successful: Starting when they are as yet unable to throw a ball, boys are not only taught to be players, but to be winners. Males learn early that what society expects is winning. (Notice how long men retain and display cheap sports trophies.)
3. Aggressive: Americans tend to disapprove of the Asian concept of *losing face*, but from the time they are little boys, American males are taught never to run away from a fight if their cause is right.
4. Sexual: Men pass down the idea that a real man—a real male—is willing and able to react and act sexually at any time.
5. Self-Reliant: The "real man" is not dependent on anybody else, and certainly not to any female anybody else. Independence, toughness, and willingness to survive alone are valued.

Towery (1992) suggested that unspoken standards of masculine behavior are taught and learned as a "male code" almost from the moment of birth:
1. Compete and win against other males who are perceived as competitors or threats.
2. Be confident, powerful, silent, and strong.
3. Talk about facts, not feelings, and do not reveal private thoughts.
4. Dominate relationships.
5. Worth comes through work.
6. Success and performance attract females.

Table 1 presents an edited comparison of these four models. Horizontal comparisons suggest that there is considerable consensus about the standards that young males may feel obligated to emulate.

TABLE 1
Four Versions of Aspects of Masculinity

Doyle	Cicone and Ruble	Brannon	Towery
Antifeminine	—	No Sissy Stuff	Talk facts, not feelings
Successful	Active and achievement oriented	The Big Wheel	Work equals worth, so produce
Aggressive	Dominant	Give Em Hell!	Action not talk; compete and win
Sexual	—	—	Performance is expected
Self-Reliant	Level headed	The Sturdy Oak	Confident, silent, strong

CHALLENGES FOR COUNSELORS

These points of view on masculinity leave us with an ironic situation: The individual male seems to be dependent on others, not himself, for the validation of his masculinity. If, as the previous observers contend, a man wants to be perceived as masculine in our North-American culture, he has to be capable of displaying a wide variety of observable behaviors. Because nobody can display all of the characteristics simultaneously, and because several are inherently contradictory and dysfunctional, validating one's masculinity becomes a complicated challenge.

In our society, for a boy to become a man he has to *do* something to pass from one category to another. Every young male has to decide how to convince himself, and those he thinks are watching, that he is no longer a little boy. The first and perhaps easiest action for the young boy to take is to loudly and conspicuously reject anything that is associated with females. He may not yet know what masculine behavior is, so in the meantime he defines it by default: Masculine must be the opposite of feminine.

Fathers are early masculinity mentors, often presenting their son with sports equipment before the boy is out of diapers. Daddies do not seem to mind much when their son plays with "GI Joe" and his buddies because they are "action figures." However, if daddy discovers his little boy playing with Barbie's friend Ken, that is usually defined as "playing with dolls," and is sometimes perceived as sufficient justification to instigate distraction techniques.

This may explain the reluctance of some young boys to resist participation in art, music, or other performing arts, and the technique some adults use in attempts to control their behavior: suggest that the behavior in question is girlish or feminine.

The felt push to achieve and to be successful can be a heavy burden. "Earn good grades, high SAT scores, hold a good job, be productive." If boys are taught and learn that they are what they do, and those results are criteria for judgment, many are doomed to an inevitable shortfall.

Boys can be sensitive to falling short of not only their own expectations, but those of their parents. The old "It's not whether you win or lose but how you play the game" cliché is all too often prescribed for somebody else. Schools need to rethink the extent to which the competition model sets the atmosphere for academic and nonacademic activities. Every enterprise does not have to be fixed in advance so that it is inevitable that there will be a few winners and many losers. It is possible and desirable to plan win-win ventures, where everybody has an opportunity to gain and there are no inevitable losers.

As noted in chapter 1, males, at least through adolescence, are more physically aggressive. Any examination of contemporary schoolboy sports demonstrates the extent to which adults and peers equate physical aggressiveness with contact sports. Participation in some sports seems to confer immediate masculinity. Justified or not, there seems to be a different interpretation placed on participation in contact sports such as football and wrestling as compared with tennis and golf.

How can a boy announce to the world that he is aggressive if he does not have the body or talent to participate in rugged sports? He may engage in extreme competitiveness and become overconcerned with dominance of other people and situations. Of course, he can always fight out of uniform and in the streets, and many boys do.

The term *aggression* is most frequently applied to such behaviors as conflict, destruction, and violence. However, in other forms, it can be quite functional. Assertiveness and determination are less hostile forms of aggression, and these are usually perceived as valued characteristics.

It is ironic that society preaches sexual restraint at the same time that it promotes sexual expression. Many have decried the double standard of sly approval of active male sexuality and the rationalization that it is little more than just "sowing wild oats." Unfortunately, it seems that if a young male is anxious for some personal and peer validation of masculinity, sexual intercourse completed and announced will do. Some males believe that "making a baby" makes them a man, although there is a world of difference between siring a child and fulfilling the responsibilities of serving as its father. But for young males who do not have much experience with a father, how are they to know? At the same time, the needs of the boy who does not feel the necessity to rush into intimate relationships must be respected. He should not be overlooked as if he has some developmental deficiency.

The emotional restraint implied as a requirement for masculinity can be devastating. It is one thing to be silent and strong, level-headed, and independent. It is quite another to believe that one should never be emotional and share private feelings. When with peers, boys are more apt to *do* things than to *discuss* things. Action seems to come easier; however, with leadership, boys can learn to recognize and express their attitudes, values, and feelings.

Parents and educators all too often communicate to boys that the only emotion they should express spontaneously is anger. When a little boy feels pain or sadness, more likely than not his parents admonish him "not to cry." The cumulative weight of the burden of repressing emotions, feelings, and any tenderness or vulnerability eventually takes its toll. If taught to hide or suppress feelings when young, the boy may find it difficult years later to express his feelings toward others.

There is another criterion for masculinity not noted by the four sources cited earlier: be a conspicuous consumer. Young males in this generation are expected to acquire and conspicuously use things—an automobile that will be admired, fashionable clothing, CDs, music systems, and so on. As is shown in later chapters, acquiring these possessions is so important that jobs that compete with academics or even illegal activities become accepted means toward the goals.

The out-of-pocket costs of our so-called "free educational system" are substantial. Economic pressures often mount until the boy finds it advantageous to leave the school for full-time money-making activities.

Because most young adolescents remain in their homes, they acquire a distorted picture of economics. Because mom is still doing the laundry and preparing meals, and dad is still paying the car insurance and not charging for rent or utilities, almost all the money earned can be expended in recreational directions. Many males in their mid-teens to early twenties often have more personal disposable income than their fathers. Unfortunately, by the mid-twenties, all of that changes with a shocking recognition that one or two minimum wage, part-time jobs cannot support one independent person, let alone another and a child.

Counselors and teachers should confront early adolescents with exercises in practical personal economics. Patterns of wasteful consumption can be replaced by more permanent reinforcements of growing financial security—something that confers legitimate masculine status.

FINAL POINTS

Freud may have been onto something important when he hypothesized the Oedipus complex. Both little boys and little girls begin life dependent on a female, resulting in identification and emotional attachments.The growing female can continue this relationship, whereas the male must separate and distance himself and form a different attachment to some male figure. Hotelling and Forrest (1985) suggested that this results in female identity that is based on relationships to and connections with others, and threatened by separation. In contrast, masculine identity becomes based on separation and is threatened by intimacy.

This rule of thumb is worth remembering: The stronger the boy's own misgivings about his masculinity, the more extreme may be the behavior he feels he must display to prove it to himself and the significant others in his social surroundings. Extreme behaviors may be a cry for internal and external confirmation of masculinity, and it can be overdone. Pittman (1990) pointed out that "heavy doses of masculinity are unquestionably toxic" (p. 42).

The challenge for counselors is to be alert for such cries, interpret them accurately, and help the boy find constructive and effective ways to acquire this status without being destructive to himself or others.

REFERENCES

Bem, S. L. (1976). Probing the promise of androgyny. In G. K. Kaplan & J. P. Bean (Eds.), *Beyond sex-role stereotypes: Readings toward a psychology of androgyny* (pp. 48–62). Boston: Little, Brown.

Bem, S. L. (1978). *Bem inventory*. Palo Alto, CA: Consulting Psychologist Press.

Brannon, R. (1976). The male sex role: Our culture's blueprint of manhood, and what it's done for us lately. In D. David & R. Brannon (Eds.), *The forty-nine percent majority* (pp. 1–45). Reading, MA: Addison-Wesley.

Cicone, M., & Ruble, D. (1978). Beliefs about males. *Journal of Social Issues, 34,* 5–16.

Doyle, J. A. (1989). *The male experience* (2nd ed.). Dubuque, IA: Wm. C. Brown.

Holland, J. L. (1985). *Vocational Preference Inventory (VPI) 1985 Revision.* Odessa, FL: Psychological Assessment Resources.

Hotelling, K., & Forrest, L. (1985). Gilligan's theory of sex-role development: A perspective for counseling. *Journal of Counseling and Development, 64,* 183–186.

Pittman, F. (1990). The masculine mystique. *The Family Therapy Networker, 14,* 40–49.

Pleck, J.H. (1981). *The myth of masculinity.* Cambridge, MA: The MIT Press.

Streiker, L. (1989). *Fathering–old game, new rules.* Nashville, TN: Abingdon Press.

Towery, T. L. (1992). *Male code: Rules men live and love by.* Lakewood, CO: Glenbridge Publishing.

CHAPTER 3

SEXUALITY: DEVELOPMENT, AWARENESS, AND EXPRESSION

One of the basic ironies of the counseling profession is that data have not been obtained for the truly important questions. Certainly this applies to adolescent sexuality. The principal reason we do not know all we would like to know about this topic is that realities of our society make collecting such information awkward and difficult.

Nevertheless, in recent years, a number of investigations have produced islands of insight within this sea of ignorance. Patterns and trends of behavior are coming into focus. Male adolescent sexuality is considered here under four categories: sexual awareness, heterosexual activity, gay and lesbian sexual activity, and teenage fathers.

SEXUAL AWARENESS

Puberty is a biological earthquake that forever alters the landscape of the physiology and psychology of the male. Sometime within a few months of the 12th year of life, a surge of testosterone enters the boy's bloodstream, triggering a chaotic cluster of structural and functional changes.

External sex organs increase in size, and pubic hair and whiskers sprout. Rapid growth in weight and height is common. Voices first crack, then change. Extremities grow first, resulting in hands, feet, noses, and ears out-distancing surrounding structures. When bones lengthen before muscles, temporary awkwardness and clumsiness often result. Oil glands in the skin overproduce, and complexions are dotted with "zits."

Sexual arousal, defined as erection accompanied by sexual feelings, occurs for the median boy sometime between his 11th and 12th birthday (95% before age 13), usually triggered by a visual stimulus (Koth, Boyd, & Singer, 1988). Then begins a period of intense, sometimes disturbing, distracting, untimely, and embarrassing responses several times a day. Another harbinger of puberty is the spontaneous discharge of semen during the night, often accompanied by erotic fantasies: the infamous, notorious "wet dream." With sexual awareness comes the discovery of its pleasures, usually beginning with sexual relief through masturbation.

Masturbation by adolescent males is apparently universal. In contrast to females, it is not unusual for boys to talk about it with other boys, to make jokes, to boast of newfound powers and pleasures, and even to engage in the practice together in a spirit of youthful camaraderie. Such activity may be misinterpreted by the boy and/or concerned adults as symptoms of homosexuality, rather than developmentally normal exploratory behavior.

Cultural stereotypes of young males lusting for heterosexual intercourse reveal much about those making the assumptions. Because male puberty arrives, on average, 2 years later than for females in our society, adolescents of the same chronological age may be differentially interested and active in heterosexual activities. Young males are not necessarily more sexually aggressive; many are content to discharge their energies via sports, cars, jobs, and traditional male-bonding activities. Sexual tensions can be and are easily relieved in the absence of female companionship. The idea that males are more erotic is a fairly recent social perception, surfacing in Victorian times. Previous to that, in literature going back as far as the Bible, men were considered less sexual (Doyle, 1989). Fortunately, the transition from boy to man eventually occurs for almost every male, and nonsolitary sexual behavior begins.

There appears to be about a 2-year developmental lag between males and females until the males catch up in their early twenties. In many high school romantic couples, the boy is a grade or two ahead and a year or two older. Many such romances crash when he goes off to college because, by that time, he is mature enough to interact with girls nearer his own age.

CHALLENGES FOR COUNSELORS

Boys moving through the stage of sexual awareness have many concerns that if not addressed can be developmentally vexing. Differential maturity is a potential source of serious problems stemming from the cruel way preadolescents treat their peers who are early or late maturers. For males, early development is an advantage for those who want to make themselves into athletic gladiators. Unfortunately for many, there often remains a little psychological boy within the body of the mesomorphic man. Late maturing males sometimes experience suffering that often affects their personalities forever. They are laughed at in the shower room, bullied on the bus, and frequently become the class clowns in order to survive.

Abnormality can be defined as a discrepancy between a situation that one expects and one that is actually experienced. Boys often worry about genital size, height and weight, spontaneous erections, wet dreams, and masturbation. How are they supposed to know that all this will pass? Years later they may look back at these years, smile, and understand, but in the meantime a great deal of unnecessary suffering can occur.

School policies and activities are not always facilitating. Such differential sexual maturity creates stresses and strains in school activities. For example, junior high school boys are usually less interested in dances than are junior high girls. When the school has a rule prohibiting older boys from attending closed school social events, the girls are trapped in the gym with a bunch of silly immature little boys who would rather be elsewhere playing video games. Hence, the girls reluctantly dance with each other while the boys play tag and devour the refreshments.

In a perfect world, families, churches, and community agencies would assume the responsibility for helping boys through this stage of development. Nevertheless, the school, and especially the school counselor, is obligated to foster the well-being of each and every student as an individual. A school that believes in developmental guidance must accept its responsibility to make available reliable and valid information about the onset of sexual awareness through group and individual services.

HETEROSEXUALITY

Substantial research evidence supports the generalization that adolescent male heterosexual activity begins earlier and is more frequent than most adults think. It has been common practice to use the phrase "sexually active" as a synonym for having heterosexual intercourse. The facts are, of course, that there are a great number of alternative nonintercourse sexual behaviors. Solo masturbation is far and away the most common and frequent expression of sexuality (Sladkin, 1985). At least 40% of adolescents participate in partner masturbation (Coles & Stokes, 1985). Oral sex was reported by 69% of a sample of teenagers who were sexually involved with a partner (Newcomer & Udry, 1985). Restricting the discussion of heterosexual activity to intercourse has several unintended consequences. First, it results in an underestimation of heterosexual interactions. Second, it continues the myth that sexual intercourse is the only way to act on sexual feelings with someone of the opposite sex. Third, it may accelerate the decision for intercourse in the absence of knowledge of alternatives.

Much research data focus on heterosexual intercourse almost exclusively. Many report total data for both sexes, some report for each sex. Orr, Wilbrandt, Brack, Raunch, and Ingersoll (1989) reported the results of a comprehensive health behavior research study conducted in an Indiana suburban, working-class, 77% White junior high school, Grades 7–9. Sexual intercourse experience was anonymously acknowledged by 70% of the boys. The frequency of boys reporting heterosexual experience by age was:

12	36.0%
13	52.7%
14	60.1%
15	73.6%
16	90.0%

Pleck ("Lifeline. Boys' Life," 1989) found that teen boys were more sexually active in 1989 than in 1979. When a national sample of males ages 15–19 were asked if they had had sexual intercourse in the past year, 76% replied yes—up from 65% in 1979.

In a Search Institute survey of 46,000 public school students in 1989–1990, Williams (1990) reported that 62% of 11th and 12th graders reported having sexual intercourse at least once.

Painter (1992) reported data from a 1990 survey of 11,631 high school students by the Centers for Disease Control (CDC). In a follow-up to an earlier report that found half of the students sexually experienced by age 16, this study found a third of the boys were experienced by age 15 with multiple partners. The percentages of boys reporting having sex with four or more partners were:

18.9% of all 9th-grade boys
38.5% of all 12th-grade boys

37.8% of African-American boys
15.8% of White boys
16.5% of Hispanic boys

Peterson (1991) reported data from a study conducted by Elizabeth McAnarney for the Urban Institute. Sexual intercourse activity among 15-year-olds rose by 50% between 1981 and 1991. Among the findings were:

60% of 15- to 19-year-old males have had sex at least once
75% of all adolescent males in 1988 were nonvirgins
17- to 19-year-old males reported an average of six different sexual partners, and intercourse an average of three times a week

Redmon (1992), a midwestern physician and gynecologist, surveyed 150 juniors in a rural Indiana county seat town. She discovered that one half of the males were having sexual intercourse.

The CDC conducts a Youth Risk Behavior Surveillance System that periodically measures the prevalence of health-risk behaviors among youth in the nation. Data from their 1990 survey indicated that male high school students were significantly more likely than female students to have had sexual intercourse and to be sexually active, which was defined as having had sexual intercourse during the 3 months preceding the survey. Both statistics increased significantly by grade of student from 9th through 12th grade. African-American students reported significantly more activity than White or Hispanic students (Centers for Disease Control, 1990).

The 1991 CDC survey produced dramatically different results. Fewer males reported ever having had sexual intercourse, but more of those who did were sexually active.

More girls reported having had sexual intercourse, and many more of them reported that they were sexually active (Centers for Disease Control, 1992). Table 1 is a comparison of these findings.

TABLE 1

Variable	1990	1991
Ever had sexual intercourse		
Boys	60.8%	57.0%
Girls	48.0%	51.0%
Yes, in past 3 months		
Boys	42.5%	64.0%
Girls	36.4%	75.0%

A final bit of indirect evidence comes from the medical world, where it has been reported that the rate of sexually transmitted diseases of teenagers is twice that of young adults in their twenties (Adler, 1993).

What are we to make of all this? Probably that junior and senior high school counselors, teachers, and youth workers can safely and confidently assume that the overwhelming majority of their male clients are sexually active, each one probably practicing masturbation and a majority experienced in willing, voluntary, consenting sexual intercourse. All of them? Probably not. Most of them? Absolutely. Adults may not approve, but the first step in managing a situation is to acknowledge that it exists. Adolescent males are definitely sexually active by themselves and/or with females.

Before condemning teenagers of today, it should be remembered that sexual activity at this age has a long American tradition. In conservative and Puritanical Concord, Massachusetts, one third of all children born during the 20 years prior to the American Revolution were conceived out of wedlock. During the 1780s and 1790s, one third of all brides in rural New England were pregnant on their wedding day. In 19th-century America, the "age of consent" for girls in many states was as low as 9 or 10 (Coontz, 1992).

CHALLENGES FOR COUNSELORS

Despite overwhelming evidence of the need, as well as mountains of evidence of the consequences of ignoring the issue, sexuality education remains a controversial issue. By their very nature, schools are conservative institutions, and their governance model ensures that they are vulnerable to attacks by groups who prefer a fantasy perception on reality. Within this arena, the counselor can play a difficult, but influential role. The dilemmas are numerous.

Critics charge that if sexuality is acknowledged and discussed in school, that very action legitimizes approval of sexual interactions. As has been demonstrated, overt sexual behavior among teens is already almost universal, but there are those who are more comfortable pretending that adolescents are sexually neutral. Schools present the facts about communism without approval or advocacy. Certainly sexuality and sexual expression can be presented in a way that neither condemns nor advocates practicing the behaviors.

Sexuality education can be successful. When Family Health International studied the World Health Organization's review of 19 scientific studies of sex education in schools, they found a consensus that: (a) sex education is most likely to be successful when given to youths who have not yet begun sexual activity, (b) sex education does not lead to earlier involvement in sex, and (c) sex education does lead to greater use of contraception (*Bottom Line*, 1994).

Differential development is a problem because not all adolescents are ready to learn the same things at the same time. If issues are raised far in advance of puberty, schools are criticized for "putting ideas into their minds." If schools wait until nearly everyone has passed puberty, the messages arrive far too late for many.

Sexuality education cannot be an event—it must be an ongoing process. A unit in a health class is insufficient. The curriculum must periodically address sexuality issues in a sequence that is in harmony with developmental progress of both sexes. In addition to group activities, adolescents must have access to adults who are approachable, knowledgeable, and open to the former's questions and concerns.

Sexuality education is not and cannot be the exclusive responsibility of the schools. Institutions like the family, the church, and the media must not only accept their role and responsibility, but be held accountable for making positive contributions to the process. Most educators would be delighted if such matters were addressed satisfactorily in the home or by churches, but neither of these social institutions have demonstrated willingness or effectiveness in this area of concern. It becomes a school issue by default.

The counselor must be able to help adolescents as they struggle to understand and express their sexuality. If the counselor is uncomfortable, clients will know. If the counselor is judgmental, clients will know. In time, such issues will cease to be presented problems as the student "grapevine" diverts help-seekers to other sources, which are not always the most valid and reliable sources of assistance. Kiselica and Pfaller (1993) presented a comprehensive overview of strategies, approaches, and services that could and should be offered to teenagers of both sexes.

Peer pressure is a problem. By nature, adolescents are prone to follow perceived peer norms. Many adolescent boys begin sexual intercourse at an early age for a secondary reason: a perception that it is an expected behavior, and the fear of being different from peers. Adults must find ways to communicate that, although many adolescent males do have sexual intercourse with females, many do not, and that this course of action is normal, acceptable, and wise.

The problem must be kept in perspective. One who gets facts only from the media might come to the conclusion that this problem is getting worse. The facts may lead us in another direction. The highest rate of teenage childbearing was in 1957: 97 per 1,000 females ages 15–19. In 1983, the rate was 52 per 1,000. (Many of these women are now the grandmothers of today's teenage girls; one would hope that their attitudes on sexuality education are liberal.) The media also tend to use ages 12-19 as the teenage era, and single out 12-year-olds as examples. In fact, only 2% of all births to teenagers occur to girls under age 15 (Vinovskis, 1988).

TEENAGE FATHERS

Teen fathers are victims of massive misunderstanding and discrimination from nearly everybody who comes into contact with them. They are simultaneously rejected and ignored, disparaged and excluded, condemned and punished. To add insult to injury, the role they actually play in the high rate of births among teenage females is considerably overestimated.

Folklore, Tall Tales, Exaggerations, and Lies
Several generalizations about teenage fathers have been identified by Robinson (1988). To paraphrase and summarize, teenage fathers are perceived as: (a) more knowledgeable about sex and sexuality, (b) exploiters of naive and defenseless females, (c) driven to prove their masculinity by making a baby, (d) only minimally affectionate toward either mother or child, and (e) possessing an attitude toward parenthood that consists of little more than a disappearing act that forces the mother and child to survive as best they can. Each of these items probably can be documented by anecdotal knowledge of a single case; but as generalizations, they are myths—untrue beliefs that are being dispelled by a growing body of evidence (Kiselica, Stroud, Stroud, & Rotzein, 1992; Robinson, 1988; Staples, 1991).

Apparently teen fathers know little more than nonteen fathers or their female partners about sexuality and reproduction (Barret & Robinson, 1982). The perception of the aggressively sexual male seducing the reluctant and naive female is a stereotype. Females can also be sexually aggressive. Most teen pregnancies are the consequence of voluntary, consenting sexual intercourse between willing partners.

There is no significant evidence that young males who become fathers are any more unsure of their masculinity than peers who have not fathered children. Most teen fathers remain involved in the lives of their partners throughout pregnancy and birth (Panzarine & Elster, 1983). Two individuals are accomplices to every pregnancy. Both should fulfill the responsibilities of parenthood. Perhaps even more young fathers would share in these experiences if they were permitted to do so, but, as has been pointed out elsewhere, teen fathers are often banished from the vicinity of their pregnant partners. Scott (1986) found that his sample of African-American fathers did make contributions up to the level of the financial responsibility they could assume. He found them willing to contribute more than they did, but were not able to do so either because of their lack of employment or their low income from the employment they could find.

Today, the separation of the young father and mother-to-be is more of an economic phenomenon than anything else. The pregnant female is often forced to continue living with her parents because of health-insurance coverage and the cost of independent housing. A teen father can hardly support a young family on a minimum-wage fast-food job. In those cases where it is economically feasible, adolescent males can make fine young husbands and fathers.

Overestimation of Numbers
Teenage boys have been lambasted for careless, wanton, and irresponsible sexual behavior resulting in unplanned pregnancies by teenage girls. Such charges are unwarranted. Census data reported by Males (1993) show that most teen pregnancies now involve 18- or 19-year-old females and males in their early twenties. In 1988, 69% of the male partners of married and unmarried teen mothers were over the age of 20, 15% older than 25. Among married teenage girls, 71% had spouses over age 20. Fatherhood rates among teenage boys peaked in 1970, and declined 20% through 1988.

In a follow-up report, Males (1994) presented more compelling evidence to show that a huge majority of teenage pregnancies are caused by male adults, not teenage boys. A 1990 analysis of 60,000 births to teenage mothers in California showed that senior high school boys fathered only 24% of all births to school-age girls. Men older than high school age fathered all the rest; they averaged nearly 4 years older than the teenage mothers. Additional confirmation comes from the National Center for Health Statistics' *1988 Vital Statistics of the United States*—data that show that only 29% of 309,819 babies born to teenage mothers that year had teenage fathers.

Becklund (1993) reported the results of a 3-month study in Los Angeles where nearly half of the young fathers who got teenage girls pregnant were ages 20–24; only 28% of them were teens themselves. On average, teen mothers have been found to be 2 years younger than the father of their child (Children's Defense Fund, 1988).

The misfortune of becoming "parents too soon" has more to do with poverty; low birth weights; and lack of minimal nutritional and health care, housing, and jobs than with morality. After all, women in their teens have been having babies in America for generations. This can be confirmed by examining almost anybody's family tree. Pregnancies in the early teens are a tragedy for everyone involved, but to make no differentiation between a pregnant 13-year-old and an expecting 19-year-old seems unwarranted.

In summary, there is no reason to believe that teenage boys today are responsible for more than about a quarter to a third of all teenage pregnancies. That is still too many, but the facts place the problem in a different perspective, and suggests different strategies.

The 22-year-old male who unintentionally fathered a baby with a 17-year-old girl should have been taught, and should have learned, sexual responsibility years ago when he was a teenager.

CHALLENGES FOR COUNSELORS

Although the number of teen fathers may be fewer than many think, there are many teenage boys today who have fathered a baby. They comprise an ignored subpopulation that needs and deserves appropriate guidance and counseling attention and services.

Perhaps a change in nomenclature would be helpful. In recent times, we have been told that the term *chairman* is sexist, and that the more generic term *chairperson* is more politically correct. Perhaps it is now time to stop using the term *teenage father* and start using *adolescent male co-parent*. That would be at least verbal recognition of co-responsibility for the creation of the child and for shared parenting responsibilities.

A review of our practices and procedures to identify, modify, and reduce punitive discrimination would seem to be in order. Society now treats the adolescent male co-parent the way it treated teenage mothers a generation ago. He is assumed to be the aggressor in the relationship, blamed for the pregnancy, removed from participation in school activities, and excluded from decisions about abortion and adoption. Parents who previously had very lax rules for their daughters now establish strict rules such as curfews, and not infrequently banish the young father-to-be from the premises.

Counselors of both sexes should take great care not to show more compassion for and understanding of the problems of the teen mother than for the teen father. Both need understanding, support, and services.

Seeking, implementing, and completing preventive actions and programs is always preferable to waiting for the management, remediation, and repair stage. The fact that most fathers of babies born to teenage girls are in their twenties does not change the fact that they were once in school, in their teens, and forming their attitudinal, value, and behavioral standards.

Which teenage boys seem to be at greatest risk of fathering a child by age 20? Obviously every male who completes sexual intercourse is at risk of fathering a child. The data from the U.S. Office of Education study suggest that there are some identifiable subpopulations that might warrant first and early attention (Center for Statistics, 1986). This large and comprehensive study was conducted using the "high school and beyond" data as a starting point (Hanson, Morrison, & Ginsburg, 1989). It was discovered that the most cogent factors predicting later teenage fathering were: being African-American, going steady, and having unorthodox views of parenting outside of marriage. Why this tends to be true is as yet unknown because, as Staples (1991) pointed out, African-American sexuality is neglected in the literature.

The adolescent males who became fathers were likely to be African-American, reside in the south, have mothers with low levels of education, exhibit academic and behavioral problems in school, possess a pessimistic outlook about their own future, and consider teen fatherhood as early as the sophomore year. Many of these factors can be changed through education and counseling.

Somewhat surprisingly, other factors did not predict. Living in a single-parent or low-income family, working mothers, large families, religious values, and completing a sex-education class did not make much difference.

All young males need developmental guidance information about maturation, normal changes and functioning, and responsible sexuality. Group guidance activities at the junior high and middle school levels could do much to dispel ignorance and misinformation. Health- and physical-education teachers have an important role to play. To expect counselors to shoulder this responsibility alone is unreasonable, but they can provide leadership. Counselors can help update school policies and curriculum, organize and deliver appropriate preventive educational experiences, and provide individual and group counseling.

Counseling services needed by teen fathers vary with the stage of the partner's pregnancy. Decisions will be made, by drift and default if not by design, because not to decide is to decide.

The counselor should not be surprised if establishing rapport with teen fathers is difficult. The stresses of the situation and the nature of recent interactions with adults logically generate resistance and defensiveness. Creating a safe atmosphere of acceptance, understanding, and trust must remain the initial goal of the counselor. It is likely that the boy will have already heard the scoldings and lectures.

In the earliest phase, both future parents face issues of notifying parents, peers, and school officials. Medical referral is a must. Next comes a barrage of decisions that must be made in a relatively short period of time: Marriage? Adoption, abortion, or parenthood? What role will and can the young man play in determining the best courses of action? New and revised relationships must be established with parents, peers, employers, and school officials. In the latter stages of pregnancy, there are issues of jobs, financial management, child care, and housing. Those teens who believed that having a child would automatically confer adult status soon discover that adulthood is more complex, demanding, and stressful than they imagined.

GAY MALE SEXUAL ORIENTATION

Homosexuality has replaced communism as the "hot-button" issue guaranteed to stir passionate discussion, debate, and alarm. When the gentle and insightful comic strip "For Better or For Worse" devoted a few weeks to a story line about a friend of the son dealing with his sexual orientation, many newspapers refused to publish it, pulpits resonated with passionate protests, conservative talk shows had a field day, and indignant epistles bombarded "Letters to the Editor." All this before most of the strips had been published.

Although gay men have served their country honorably in many wars, and thousands have sacrificed their lives, a proposal to prohibit discrimination on the basis of status rather than overt conduct met with such a fire storm of protest that President Clinton decided to adopt a compromise stance. Logic, science, compassion, and rationality sometimes flies out the window when ideas become too threatening. When Edward Jenner began vaccination against smallpox, some newspapers printed fanciful woodcut depictions of babies with bovine features supposedly born by vaccinated mothers.

A Definition.
Gay male and lesbian sexual orientation can be defined as a consistent and characteristic attraction to and a preference for sexual interaction with individuals of the same sex. It has been commonplace throughout history, and even in America as late as Victorian times it was "not an issue." It is today.

Yes, No, or Maybe?
A young boy should not and cannot be considered gay as a result of a single or even a few sexual contacts with another male. Occasionally a young male discovers what homosexuality is and then matches it with an incident from his past, which seems to fit the definition. Isolated instances of same-sex contacts ranging from sexual arousal to orgasm are common episodes in the normal growing-up experiences of many, if not most, adolescents. Such exploratory, playful, or even hazing incidents are insufficient evidence of gay male sexual orientation.

However, some young males discover in their early teens that they are indeed gay. For most it is as much a surprise to them as it will be later to family and friends.

Why?
Nobody knows for sure why one person becomes heterosexual and another gay. Speculations have included defective parenting, insufficient male role models, possession by devils, something learned, some-

thing mislearned, something chosen, or something traceable to genetic predestination.

Some say "why" is unimportant, but as long as our understanding is primitive and fragmentary there will be room for erroneous and hurtful explanations. For example, some believe that gay male sexual orientation is a chosen life-style—a preference—and gay men are what they are because they were recruited, taught, and persuaded to alter their basic heterosexual tendencies. "By definition they don't reproduce themselves, so it should be obvious that they seduce and recruit new members." This cluster of beliefs leads to worry about adult gay men and lesbians preying upon otherwise heterosexual children. Gay male and lesbian sexual orientation is perceived as an evil, immoral choice. (This point of view overlooks the fact that if there was a $10-million bounty paid to anyone who could parent a baby boy to the status of an adult gay man or lesbian, nobody would have the slightest idea of how to do it.)

Another perspective suggests that homosexuality is a naturally occurring and common variation—that gay men and lesbians do not choose to be who they are, but simply develop that way. Like being left-handed, homosexuality is thought to develop from a cluster of genetic possibilities triggered by currently unknown and unidentified factors and forces.

Some recent preliminary work by a team of geneticists suggests that there may be a genetic predisposition that influences homosexual expression. These scientists found that gay males not only have unusually high numbers of gay brothers, but also many uncles and cousins, but only in their mothers' families. Their careful analysis of DNA samples resulted in a finding that there appears to be a gene site on the X chromosome that possibly contributes to homosexual orientation (Pool, 1993). If supported by further research, such a finding would have profound social implications.

Magnitude and Frequency
How many young males are gay? The best answer is that we do not know because seeking such information has been difficult, if not forbidden. For many years, the Kinsey (1948) estimate (from data collected from volunteers and prisoners in mid-1940s) that 10% of males are gay was widely quoted and accepted. Recent data gathered in France and Great Britain place the estimate at no more than half that level. Lyon and Fila (1992) reported that the latest data collected

by the National Opinion Research Center at the University of Chicago showed a homosexual incidence of about 4%.

Using a compromise estimate of 5% means that, for every 100 students in a school, perhaps as many as 5 are gay; in a school of 1,000, as many as 50; and so forth. Certainly every school is likely to have a number sufficient to deserve appropriate attention and services from those people who are there to be sensitive and respond to problems and needs. Because males report awareness of their homosexual feelings at an average age of 13, and first act on those feelings at an average age of 15 (Bell, Weinberg, & Hammersmith, 1981), those events will take place during the junior and senior high school years.

Unique Needs

Gay adolescent males face two categories of stress: inner conflicts related to coming to terms with their sexual nature, and external challenges and threats from individuals and society (Hall & Fradkin, 1992).

Identity and self-esteem issues. Adolescence is, by definition, a time for the construction and clarification of the self-concept. Erikson (1963) wrote that finding one's identity and developing intimacy with another individual are central tasks of adolescence and early adulthood. Coming to terms with one's sexuality is an integral part of these challenges.

Interpersonal and peer relationship issues. The young man may withdraw from usual peer relationships in an attempt to diminish perceived consequences of discovery. He may disguise his private feelings by conspicuous heterosexual dating, contact sports, and/or aggressive and antisocial acts. He may reject and flee from any association with the performing arts such as drama, music, art, or dance. The burden of maintaining a false persona can result in psychological stress, maladjustment, and troubled interpersonal relationships.

Personal safety issues. Homophobia is the term used to describe the extreme feelings of threat perceived by some heterosexuals, frequently followed by acts of verbal aggression and physical violence towards those they perceive to be gay. In schools, this is exhibited by taunting, ridicule, and physical beatings, usually involving multiple aggressors. One study concluded that 45% of gay males experience verbal and/or physical assaults in high school (Eaton, 1993).

Self-harm issues. Some young gay men engage in a variety of self-destructive activities that puzzle the adults who care about them.

Academic performance may deteriorate, alcohol and/or drug abuse may develop, and thoughts of self-destruction can lead to suicide attempts. Kournay (1987) surveyed 66 adolescent psychiatrists and reported that a majority of them considered gay adolescents at higher risk for suicide, and agreed that the suicidal gestures and attempts were more likely to be serious, not theatrical. Coleman and Remafedi (1989) claimed that as many as a third of gay adolescents have attempted suicide. A U.S. Department of Health and Human Services (HHS) survey concluded that gay and lesbian youth account for about one third of all successful teen suicides, and are two to three times more likely to attempt self-destruction (Eaton, 1993).

Family issues. Many parents have problems in accepting and acknowledging the heterosexuality of their children. To accept and acknowledge the gay sexual orientation of a son is almost more than some parents can bear. Although he may have hidden his homosexuality from parents for threat of rejection, punishment, or expulsion from the family, parents can perceive this as a conspiracy to keep them uninformed. Their embarrassment and anger often seek a target, and anybody in the vicinity will do, including the school counselor. They may charge a breach of communication, demand identification of causes, or insist on some form of sexual expression-conversion therapy.

Home life for young gay adolescents can become so stressful that many leave home prematurely because of the intensity of conflicts with parents. In one study, about half of gay students claimed they were rejected by their parents, and the HHS study cited previously revealed that 26% felt forced to leave home because of family conflicts over their sexual identity.

Mental health issues. It is ironic that gay adolescent males are called *gay* when so many are struggling to overcome private terrors of confusion, shame, guilt, fear, and unhappiness. Many are torn apart emotionally, physically, and spiritually. Mistrustful and afraid, feelings of alienation and isolation can develop, resulting in such psychological defenses as denial, repression, reaction formation, sublimation, and rationalization.

CHALLENGES FOR COUNSELORS

Few adolescent males bounce into their counselor's office blurting out that they want to discuss aspects of their emerging sexuality that are causing distress. When the problem is homosexuality, rather than heterosexuality, such an opening is even less likely.

Sometimes clients—unsure, ambivalent, or actually afraid of where disclosure may lead—put forth a less volatile issue as a test of the counselor's professionalism. Others are unaware of the underlying theme that is beginning to manifest itself in so many aspects of their private and interpersonal world. Schneider and Tremble (1986) pointed out one reason why communication is so often difficult:

> Homosexual feelings can be difficult to identify and articulate. Teenagers tend to believe that they have invented everything for the first time. Thus, without vocabulary to articulate homosexual feelings a youngster often believes no one else in the world feels that way. (p. 77)

This is the stage of counseling where patience and listening skills are absolutely necessary. Creating an environment where boys can feel safe enough to explore threatening ideas is what counselors do best. The challenges are to accept, listen, detect what is only inferred, and see and feel their world from their perspective.

The counselor must neither underreact by immediately dismissing such concerns as little more than a temporary developmental phase nor overreact by communicating alarm and disapproval. If the counselor is unable to work appropriately with gay clients, then standards of ethical professional behavior mandate that referral sources be utilized.

Verbal slurs, epithets, and physical assaults against gay students are often tolerated in schools in a way that profanity and racial slurs are not. Such harassments are probably in violation of the Education Amendments of 1972, Title VII of the Civil Rights Act, and the Equal Protection Clause of the Fourteenth Amendment. In 1992, the U.S. Supreme Court ruled that a school can be forced to pay damages to victims of sexual harassment. If for no other reason than the threat of huge legal bills and damage awards, schools must face and resolve this issue.

To conclude with a reminder that homosexuality is a controversial subject is almost unwarranted. Nevertheless, it is an issue that is unlikely to remain dormant much longer. Because it is always better to be proactive than reactive, counselors should lend their support to any local effort that seems to be a logical, timely, and appropriate response. This situation will not disappear by a conspiracy of silence and pretense that it does not exist.

To summarize, by its very definition, *adolescence* is the stage of life when young males become sexually expressive. It is an occurrence that forcefully demands attention, regardless of whether the individual feels ready and sufficiently prepared.

Often counselors say goodbye to a little boy for the summer, only to greet a young man several pounds heavier, several inches taller, and in need of a shave 3 months later. His behavioral changes are just as dramatic, if not just as apparent. What may not have changed is that, in many ways, a little boy still resides within that young man.

Directly and indirectly, schools can help young males understand this new dimension of their lives, and to develop modes of expression that lay the foundation for mature and responsible male adulthood.

REFERENCES

Adler, T. (1993, April). Sense of invulnerability doesn't drive teen risks. *APA Monitor, 43,* p. 15.

Barret, R. L., & Robinson, B. E. (1982). A descriptive study of teenage expectant fathers. *Family Relations, 31,* 349–352.

Becklund, L. (1993, March 14). I wanted somebody to love. *The Los Angeles Times,* pp. E1, 4, 5.

Bell, A.P., Weinberg, M.S., & Hammersmith, S. K. (1981). *Sexual preference: Its development in men and women.* Bloomington, IN: Indiana University Press.

Bottom Line. (1994, February 1). 3, 7.

Centers for Disease Control. (1990). *Chronic disease and health promotion reprints from the MMWR: 1990 youth risk behavior surveillance system.* Atlanta, GA: Author.

Centers for Disease Control. (1992). *Selected behaviors that increase risk for HIV infection, other sexually transmitted diseases, and unintended pregnancy among high school students—United States, 1991.* Atlanta, GA: Author.

Center for Statistics.(1986). *High school and beyond. 1980: Sophomore cohort second follow-up (1984). Contractor report—data file user's manual.* Washington, DC: U.S. Department of Education.

Children's Defense Fund. (1988). *Adolescent and young adult fathers: Problems and solutions.* Washington, DC: Author.

Coleman, E., & Remafedi, G. (1989). Gay, lesbian, and bisexual adolescents: A critical challenge to counselors. *Journal of Counseling and Development, 42,* 36–68.

Coles, R., & Stokes, G. (1985). *Sex and the American teenager.* New York: Harper & Row.

Coontz, S. (1992). *The way we never were.* New York: Basic Books.

Doyle, J. A. (1989). *The male experience* (2nd ed.). Dubuque, IA: Wm. C. Brown.

Eaton, S. (1993, July/August). Gay students find little support in most schools. *The Harvard Education Letter, IX,* p. 4.

Erikson, E. (1963). *Childhood and society* (2nd ed.). New York: Norton.

Hall, A., & Fradkin, R. (1992). Affirming gay men's mental health: Counseling with a new attitude. *Journal of Mental Health, 14,* 362–374.

Hanson, S. L., Morrison, D. R., & Ginsburg, A. (1989). The antecedents of teenage fatherhood. *Demography, 26,* 579–596.

Kinsey, A. C., Pomeroy, W.B., & Martin, C.E. (1948). *Sexual behavior in the human male.* Philadelphia: W.B. Saunders.

Kiselica, M. S., & Pfaller, J. (1993). Helping teenage parents: The independent and collaborative roles of counselor educators and school counselors. *Journal of Counseling & Development, 72,* 42–48.

Kiselica, M. S., Stroud, J., Stroud, J., & Rotzein, A. (1992). Counseling the forgotten client: The teen father. *Journal of Mental Health Counseling, 14*(3), 338–350.

Koth, R., Kelly, B., & Singer, B. (1988). Empirical tests of sexual selection theory: Predictions of sex differences in onset, intensity, and time course of sexual arousal. *The Journal of Sex Research, 24,* 73–89.

Kournay, R. F. C. (1987). Suicide among homosexual adolescents. *Journal of Homosexuality, 13,* 111–117.

Lifeline. Boys' life. (1989, March 31). *USA Today,* p. D1.

Lyon, J., & Fila, B. (1992, November 29). Keeping score. *Chicago Tribune Magazine,* pp. 14–47.

Males, M. (1993). Schools, society, and "teen" pregnancy. *Phi Delta Kappan, 74,* 566–568.

Males, M. (1994). Poverty, rape, adult/teen sex: Why "pregnancy prevention" programs won't work. *Phi Delta Kappan, 75,* 407–410.

National Center for Health Statistics. (1988). *Vital statistics of the United States: Vol. 1. Natality.* Hyattsville, MD: Public Health Services.

Newcomer, S. F., & Udry, J. R. (1985). Oral sex in an adolescent population. *Archives of Sexual Behavior, 14,* 41–46.

Orr, D. P., Wilbrandt, M. L., Brack, C. J., Raunch, S. P., & Ingersoll, G. M. (1989). Reported sexual behaviors and self-esteem among young adolescents. *American Journal of Diseases of Children, 143,* 86–90.

Painter, K. (1992, April 10). Teens' risky sexual behavior. *USA Today,* p. 1.

Panzarine, S., & Elster, A. B. (1983). Coping in a group of expectant adolescent fathers: An exploratory study. *Journal of Adolescent Health Care, 4,* 117–120.

Peterson, K. S. (1991, July 24). Studies show many youths aren't virgins. *USA Today,* p. 50.

Pool, R. (1993, July 16). Evidence for homosexual gene. *Science, 261,* pp. 291–292.

Redmon, C. (1992, October 16). Study shows disturbing results concerning sex habits of teens. *Associated Press* and *Terre Haute Tribune Star*, p. 8.

Robinson, B. E. (1988). *Teenage fathers.* Lexington, MA: Lexington Books.

Schneider, M., & Tremble, B. (1986). Gay or straight? Working with the confused adolescent. *Journal of Social Work and Human Sexuality, 4,* 71–82.

Scott, J. (1986). From teenage parenthood to polygamy: Case studies in black polygamous family formation. *Western Journal of Black Studies, 10,* 172–179.

Sladkin, K. (1985). Counseling adolescents about sexuality. *Seminars in Adolescent Medicine, 1,* 223–230.

Staples, R. (1991). *The black family: Essays and studies.* Belmont, CA: Wadsworth.

Vinovskis, M. (1988). *An "epidemic" of adolescent pregnancy? Some historical and policy considerations.* New York: Oxford University Press.

Williams, D. (1990, June). Teenagers' search for new connections. *Search Institute Source, VI,* pp. 1–3.

CHAPTER 4

BOYS AS STUDENTS

We know less about boys before age 5 and after age 18 than we do about them between these ages for a very simple reason: Before 5 and after 18, fewer boys are in school. Much, if not most, of what is known and understood about boys is based on observations and data collected from them in academic settings while they are students in schools. It is the best place in town to find large numbers of subjects, and the setting provides sufficient time to observe behavior and collect information.

Some of the information that has been accumulated over the years relates directly to boys' academic performance. Information about other segments of their nonstudent lives is obtained in academic settings because they can reveal it to teachers and counselors during their tenure as students. Some of the most important generalizations are followed here by a more detailed presentation of the evidence and a discussion of implications for professional practice.

THIS IS KNOWN

A considerable amount of evidence justifies at least four clusters of generalizations about what is known about boys in academic settings:

1. Boys are not without assets for academic work. They have a slightly higher quantitative aptitude, slightly lower verbal fluency. They are better at right-brain/visual spatial-relation tasks, symbol manipulation, maps and mazes, gross-motor control, and eye-hand coordination, and they are more rule bound and single-minded.
2. Boys are definitely less successful in school. They are assigned lower grades at every level of education, are more likely to be

retained in grade, are more likely to drop out before graduation, and are less likely to go on to college or earn a college
degree if they try.

3. Boys are more likely to be scolded and reprimanded for the
    same behavior that is overlooked if done by girls; they are
    more frequently disciplined, suspended, and expelled.

4. Boys are more often identified as needing special and reme-
    dial services. They comprise a majority of all students diag-
    nosed as learning disabled, educable mentally retarded, and
    behaviorally disordered. Boys are more often labeled dyslectic,
    and poor readers, and they suffer more often from delayed
    speech acquisition and stuttering. Three quarters of all those
    diagnosed with attention deficit-hyperactivity disorder (ADHD),
    the most frequent psychiatric diagnosis among American
    children, are males.

SCHOLARSHIP AND THE LACK OF IT

The fact that boys are assigned lower grades in all subjects at all
levels comes as a surprise to many, but this pattern was identified
many years ago and has been consistently documented many times.
Writing in the mid-1960s, Tyler (1965) summarized research to that
point in time and concluded that, "...all studies of *school* achievement agree that girls consistently make better school records than
boys" (p. 241, italics original). Nothing has come on the scene
since then to alter this summarization of research.

One way to verify this generalization is to go to the school records
and tabulate how many students by sex are assigned As and Bs as
contrasted with Ds and Fs, and how many girls and boys comprise
the honor society, the honor roll, and academically talented classes.
One suburban junior high school of 358 students did this and discovered that boys were awarded fewer As and Bs and more Ds and
Fs in science, social studies, English, and mathematics, and comprised a minority of the honor roll in all three grades.

Lower average grades seem inconsistent with their performance
on standardized tests. Boys tend to make higher scores in mathematics, spatial relations, and science. On the average, boys score
higher on the Scholastic Test of Academic Aptitude (SAT), American College Testing Program (ACT), Graduate Record Examination
(GRE), Medical College Admission Test (MCAT), and Graduate Man-

agement Admissions Test (GMAT). They also earn at least two thirds of all the National Merit Scholarships awarded each year (Sadker, Sadker, & Donald, 1989).

Why do boys have so many academic problems? A grade is a symbol of the extent to which the teacher is satisfied with the individual's performance and production as a student. Tyler (1965) explained that boys receive lower grades as the result of higher teacher value on docility and submissiveness. Boys are inclined to be less docile, well prepared, compliant, and neat. Such behaviors impress teachers and inflate evaluations far beyond objective subject-matter achievement. From the rationalization that academic achievement is process as well as product, it can be argued that boys receive lower grades because they deserve them.

Another hypothesis suggests that boys are caught in a severe role conflict between a society that expects them to be active, independent, and aggressive, and school norms that reward quiet behavior and obedience. Boys who score high on sex-appropriate behavior also score high on measures of anxiety.

As Moir and Jessell (1991) pointed out, "His is the world of action, exploration, and things. But school tells him to sit quiet, listen, not fidget, and pay attention to ideas; everything, in fact, that his brain and body are telling him not to do."

The competition for adolescent energy and attention has some effect on academic performance. At the secondary level, boys are more likely to engage in competitive activities such as sports and part-time jobs, which diminish time for study and homework. The competitive role of working takes time from academic activities: Many boys are unprepared for examinations and are tardy in submitting homework because they spent last night in a fast-food kitchen or at team practice rather than the library. This is discussed in greater detail in a later chapter.

Minority males struggle with academic challenges on several fronts. African-American males are twice as likely to be enrolled in special-education English classes than English classes for the gifted and talented, and are less likely to be enrolled in college-prep classes (Raspberry, 1990).

About one half of Hispanic students drop out of school before graduation, and fewer than 10% graduate from college (Schumacher, 1992). Ironically, Hispanics tend to possess many of the values that educators believe are necessary for academic success, such as loyalty to family, strong religious faith, and a sound work ethic. Unfortunately, many schools and counselors have not succeeded in establishing a minimum level of trust, communication, and cooperation with Hispanic males. To complicate this situation further, Hispanic teachers make up no more than 3% of our elementary and secondary teaching force—less than even school counselors. It is likely that remediating this oversight will become a matter of highest priority in the years ahead.

DEALING WITH DEFECTS AND DEFICIENCIES

Students who are identified as needing special education for mild learning handicaps are typically male. One estimate suggests that 85% of those in programs for learning disabilities, educable mentally retarded, and behavior disorders are boys (Phipps, 1982). Hyperactivity is diagnosed 95% more often in boys (Restak, 1979). Restless, impulsive, and easily distracted, they are more likely, in later life, to be arrested, have felony convictions, and serve time in prison (Cowley & Ramo, 1993).

Compared with girls, boys are approximately four times as likely to be diagnosed as suffering from delayed speech acquisition, infantile autism, stuttering, and dyslexia, and are about twice as likely to be classified as being mentally retarded (Harness, Epstein, & Gordon, 1984; Hier, 1979; Miedzian, 1991). African-American males comprise nearly one half of the students receiving special-education services (Raspberry, 1990).

Why are these things so? Nobody really knows, but several speculations have been put forth. One explanation is biological in nature, suggesting that the reduced space on the Y chromosome results in more sex-linked problems. Another hypothesis is that there may be a connection between the fact that more than two thirds of the nation's teachers are White females. If boys are raised, taught, disciplined, and counseled only by females, perhaps they are victims of another form of discrimination. If teachers are more sensitive to boys' behavior, then it is possible that girls also needing special services are overlooked. No conclusive evidence has surfaced.

DROPOUTS

Boys have always comprised the majority of school dropouts. When Pearl Harbor was bombed in 1941, only 25% of Americans were high school graduates. In those days, that did not matter much. Now it does.

For each 100 youngsters who enter the first grade, approximately 70 receive diplomas 12 years later. The reason that statistics on dropouts vary is because, like the unemployment percent, the drop-out rate is a *political* statistic. Those who report both have a vested interest in how the data are used. Counselors understand that un-employment statistics do not include those with a part-time job, those who did not search last week, or those underemployed. The underestimation of dropouts is standard operating procedure in most American schools. One way this is done is by changing the base figure every year—by reporting the loss from the first day of school to the last. Individual students are rarely tracked. This allows those who do not show up on Day 1 to fall through the cracks. Some Chicago school officials have reported that as many as 25% of the graduates of elementary schools never show up at high school to be identified and become a member of a base population (Lefkowitz, 1987).

Why do so many boys drop out of school before graduation when all of the conventional wisdom is that both they and society would be better if they did not? Perhaps the reasoning sequence for young men is similar to that of adults. Consider the steps an adult experi-ences before deciding to drop out of some organization.

Phase 1: He begins to sense that what's going on around him in that setting is becoming irrelevant to his interests and needs. The expected behaviors become meaningless and burdensome.

Phase 2: He begins to sense that nobody there would really miss him if he were not present, often welcoming his departure because he has recently become an irritant by becoming a nonconformist and raising awkward questions.

Phase 3: He comes to realize that there are alternative outlets for his efforts and energy—activities that more adequately meet his needs. So he severs the relationship, and does not return to the group. People of all ages sever their relationships with organizations when they sense that they do not like it anymore, and that the feeling is mutual. Almost all of us are "dropouts" from something.

The trajectory toward dropping out can be traced to the elemen-tary school years, where future dropouts begin psychological with-drawal years before departing physically. Somebody once suggested that no youngster ever rejected the school before the school rejected him or her. The unfortunate fact is that many educators are relieved when some youngsters quit school: Many who leave are troubled and troublesome, and resources for addressing those conditions are in short supply and of low priority.

Researchers from the Indiana State University School of Education conducted a state-wide investigation into dropouts from Indiana schools for the State Department of Education and General Assembly (Beymer, Hill, & Osmon, 1987). Among the items presented to a large sample of counselors, principals, and superintendents was: "For the majority of our dropouts, the school is better off after they leave." Of the superintendents, 57% agreed; of the principals, 69% agreed; and of the counselors, 63% agreed. As long as the schools are not held accountable for students who drop out, as well as those who persist, the dropout rate is likely to continue to be underestimated.

CONTROL, MANAGEMENT, AND DISCIPLINE

What educators refer to as *discipline problems* consist essentially of how strong feelings are managed. This mandates some judgment about whether the observed behavior is "normal" and expected, or "abnormal" and something to be noticed, addressed, and corrected.

Behavior is classified as *abnormal* by the observer if it deviates so much from what he or she expects to see that it bothers him or her. This places the responsibility in the eye of the beholder, and explains why opinions differ about what is and what is not worth noticing and reacting to.

Like grading, teachers selectively make decisions about what they observe and compare that with some mental image of what they expect and want to see. If the discrepancy exceeds some level, a reaction is triggered. When passing in the halls, junior high school boys often poke at each other. They frequently nervously tap their feet or a pencil, and draw attention to themselves by making what will charitably be referred to here as "rude noises." The teacher of seventh-grade boys who reacts to each and every deviation from standards of genteel behavior will be completely exhausted by the end of the first week of school.

Other behaviors are more serious. The natural and predictable behavior of older male adolescents is sometimes misunderstood by their teachers, especially female teachers. Sometimes it is interpreted as challenges to authority, or the first steps of loss of control. Sometimes sexual threats are imagined or implied. If the behavior becomes too threatening, steps are initiated to squelch it. All too often this initiates a "domino effect" of augmented conflict.

Mixed messages produce mixed reactions. Although our cultural standards urge males to be independent, aggressive, and active, in school such behavior is frequently discouraged and punished. The behavior of minority males is especially worthy of note because they are far more likely to be scolded, suspended, and expelled.

SPARKS FROM A CULTURE CLASH

African-American males face vexing dilemmas in today's schools. Despite trendy "school improvement" and "school reform" projects, African-American males still suffer massive alienation from the educational process (Lee, 1992). Much of the problem can be traced to a collision of cultural values and modes of behavior. Schools have embodied traditional White, female, middle-class standards of behavior and values. This atmosphere is dysfunctional in a multicultural society, where non-White Americans are in the majority in the 25 largest school districts in the United States (Grossman, 1991). This serious cultural mismatch is producing problems.

African-American expressiveness is a concept that refers to a cluster of behaviors that are traditional, normal, and functional in the African-American minority population, but challenging and threatening to the majority culture that establishes rules for institutional behavior (Pasteur & Toldson, 1982).

Five components, or dimensions, of characteristic cultural-expressiveness behaviors have been identified as follows:

1. High levels of emotional energy in social interactions, such as aggressive verbal interchanges and physical roughhousing.
2. Immediate, almost impulsive expression of feelings and attitudes with minimum suppression or repression.
3. Use of style and flair in expressing personality via fashion, grooming, recreation, and sports.
4. Direct, creative, noisy, and colorful communication using both oral and body language.
5. Ability to integrate thought, feeling, and movement into statements of integrated expression.

The manifestation of the behaviors listed previously can be dangerous to the academic health of an African-American teenage male because of the possibility, if not the probability, that they are often misinterpreted as being deviant, deficient, and threatening by observers. The consequences then follow the sorry sequence of anger, frustration, failure, and departure.

School officials, teachers, counselors, and administrators may be quicker to punish behaviors by African-American males because it somehow frightens the former more than the same actions by White students.

With only scattered exceptions, no American school system has demonstrated a successful model that results in high motivation and academic achievement by most African-American students. Even those with deep pockets have failed; after spending literally millions of dollars in efforts to improve the education of minorities, a prominent foundation reluctantly and sadly concluded that nothing that they had tried was really successful.

When answers are not forthcoming, perhaps it is time to ask different questions. Many have assumed that African-Americans are not doing well in school because they cannot. Poverty, single-parent homes, and drugs and alcohol are cited as excuses, if not reasons. But what if they are not doing well in school because they consciously or unconsciously choose not to do so for private reasons? This possibility is supported by recent research by an investigator who spent 4 years in the culture of a multiracial high school using the techniques of anthropology, rather than psychology.

Signithia Fordham has put forth this analysis, supported by impressive confirming evidence:

> One major reason black students do poorly in school is that they experience inordinate ambivalence and affective dissonance in regard to academic effort and success. This problem arose partly because white Americans traditionally refused to acknowledge that black Americans are capable of intellectual achievement, and partly because black Americans subsequently began to doubt their own intellectual ability, began to define academic success as white people's prerogative, and began to discourage their peers, perhaps unconsciously, from emulating white people in academic striving, i.e., "acting white." (Fordham & Ogbu, 1986, p. 177)

She found that African-American students who do succeed academically often pay a very high price (Fordham, 1988). African-American males who took many advanced-placement courses were targets of rumors that they were gay or "perverts." High-achieving males survived by being athletes, being class clowns, forming alliances with bullies, and keeping low profiles. She found that African-American males were far more confused and ambivalent about the value of forsaking their indigenous beliefs and values.

Her work suggests that, perhaps inadvertently, the school forces African-American students to deal with an intolerable dilemma: a perceived forced choice between being academically successful and being African-American. The students she observed, studied, and came to know did not believe that academic success would gain them acceptance by Whites, but they were convinced that it would alienate them from other African-American students and leave them isolated. So did many of their parents.

Although further research is needed, and is underway, the importance of this way of conceptualizing the situation should not be underestimated. If what we see is not what has to be—if it is the result of deliberate decisions—then there is a possibility that we can alter perceptions and then behaviors. If the current situation is not inevitable, that is encouraging. Change then becomes possible.

IMPLICATIONS FOR COUNSELORS

Counselors can do much to improve the educational atmosphere for boys. The first question to ask is whether some school policies are part of the problem. In medicine, over a thousand "iatrogenic diseases" have been identified—bad things that happen to people as a result of medical treatments. Hospitals do not intend to hurt anybody, but the fact is that many who go there for one reason contract new medical problems, such as staph infections and allergic reactions to medicines.

Schools do not intend to hurt students either, but many inadvertent injuries are inflicted nevertheless. School policies should be perceived as something perishable. They should have expiration dates, and near that time should be reexamined, reinstituted, modified, or discarded.

Counselors should do more local research. There are about 80,000 public schools in this country, each with its own student body personality. In some ways, national generalizations fit; in others, they do not. Counselors can provide invaluable information to decision-making groups and individuals within the school. In the age of desk-top computers and user-friendly software, the task is within the time and talent reach of all counselors.

Some data collection can be conducted by students. For example, if one takes a school yearbook to the cafeteria every day for a week, asking students if they know where last year's students are now, valuable information can be collected with no postage, printing, or data processing costs.

If a faculty wonders whether boys get significantly fewer As and Bs and more Ds and Fs, data on the premises can provide the answer. The same goes for differences in special-education diagnosis, discipline, and suspension. Sometimes the conclusion will be that no significant problems exist. Sometimes the evidence suggests that they are present. The first step in solving any problem is to decide whether a problem truly exists.

Diversity is a fact of life, and schools must be in the forefront of not only recognition, but implementation of appropriate adjustments in policies and practices. *Diversity* is not a narrow and restricted code phrase for a Hispanic, African-American, or Asiatic agenda, but includes accommodations for differences in religion, sex, social class, and other forms of status and expression.

We are all members of minorities, depending on the criterion chosen. Minorities as well as majorities have responsibilities. Being the member of a minority is neither an excuse nor a license for inappropriate behavior. Those who noisily insist that they are not understood ironically appear to not understand others themselves. We live in a complicated age of social transitions where we are all in this together.

In a time when the number of minority teachers is declining and the majority of African-American families are fatherless, it is important to find ways to identify minority male role models and get them into the schools. For example, one midwestern high school invites men to come in for academic and extraclass activities, wearing colorful lettered T-shirts. Young African-American males do not seem to realize that there are more African-American dentists in this country than African-American athletes. Interacting more with the former might be beneficial to both.

The social climate of any school must be determined within that context. It takes considerable courage to sincerely try to find out to what extent, if any, the school is seen by students as a feminine operation, or as a White-values operation. It may be discovered that the situation is not what we thought, and that certain adjustments are warranted. It is also possible that what is thought to be apathy is really satisfaction.

Counselors and teachers should become active members of curriculum reform and modification efforts. Krumboltz (1988), among others, contended that one of the basic goals of education should be to "...inspire a love of learning that will motivate a lifelong eagerness to acquire new knowledge and skills" (p. 2). He pointed out that school counselors are first and foremost educators, and occupy a key position in those deliberately created learning environments we call *schools*.

Experienced educators—teachers and counselors—understand that youngsters need to have feelings of positive self-worth, confidence, and pride in their growing accomplishments. What happens to individual students in school can help or hinder progress toward these goals. Recent books and journal articles on "school reform" have rarely mentioned the contributions counselors can make to the process. Nobody else on the faculty has a better perspective on the real needs and concerns of students. Counselors should make sure that they are represented on all committees and task forces that are assembled to improve and modernize the educational climate and curriculum of their school.

Many counselors report that it seems fashionable for teenage boys in groups to be confrontational, irreverent, rebellious, and defiant in school. This attitude is personified on the comics page of the daily newspaper in "Calvin and Hobbes" and on television by Bart Simpson. Even the "Peanuts" gang includes some popular school haters.

It is also fashionable for adults to lament "lack of respect"; but if we want respect from them, perhaps we must begin with the behavior we definitely can control—our own. Who shows disrespect first? If kids have to take care of themselves most of the time at home, if they spend more time with peers and television than with positive adult role models, how are they supposed to learn how to behave? Most of them really do want to know, if only to have something to deviate from to express independence.

Finally, counselors can help young men find private and personal reasons to extract the maximum benefits from the academic experiences the school offers. Education is predicated on the belief that sometime in the future the individual will draw on what has been learned to help acquire a desired life-style. "Work hard today, prepare yourself, postpone immediate diversions and gratifications, and get ready." In previous generations, this ethic was the driving force behind all American education. Today, it seems to have been battered considerably, and has been devalued to the status of a myth to many young men.

Unfortunately, many adolescent males today point to their relatives and acquaintances and observe that following the formula precisely does not guarantee economic security. If the goal of schooling is the acquisition of a good job, what happens when there are no good jobs available? Why postpone any form of immediate satisfaction for some vague tomorrow that may never come?

Most educators did not know at the time, but they were being raised in accordance with the Protestant work ethic; because it did pay off for us, we have difficulty when others do not seem to enthusiastically follow in our path.

Look and listen to the propaganda directed toward adolescents today. They are urged to go to school, to stay in school, and to become proficient in certain subjects in order to please politicians, the public, and the press. They hear that it is their duty to become a skilled and obedient member of the work force so the nation can win in international commerce competition. They are admonished to do all of these things for other people's reasons.

Counselors can help young men find meaning in schooling by emphasizing enlightened self-interest as the primary motivator. One of the basic laws of learning is that the person learns only what is perceived to be in his or her self-interest. The person learns much before he or she goes to school, much outside of school hours, and a lifetime of learning after formal schooling ends. Only in school does the person learn what somebody else says is important, even when he or she cannot perceive why.

It would be an error to conclude that the learner should remain passive unless he or she understands the implications and applications of what he or she is asked to learn. The lesson that counselors can reinforce is that education is a change in behavior as a result of experiences, and that it empowers the individual to make choices that could not be made otherwise.

If a male adolescent is going to accept an invitation to go swimming with the girl of his dreams, he must learn to swim. Otherwise the choice option evaporates. A young male learns to play an electric guitar, to drive a stick-shift car, and to memorize the nonrhyming lyrics of a hundred rock and roll songs without being coerced or getting a grade. He learns these things because he believes that it opens up choices otherwise not available.

Likewise, he can come to understand that if he can learn to express himself in proper oral and written English, and understand ideas expressed in the form of numbers, he will have the future job options not otherwise available.

If we transported a bus load of boys to a shopping mall and told them that they could leave that afternoon with whatever they could find inside that might be useful to them in their future, they could handle that. Why is it that we haul them to schools that have the same potential, yet they are satisfied to leave every day with little or nothing?

If every adolescent boy came to every class every day with his own private reasons for learning what is taught there, we would have a true revolution in schooling. It is worth a try.

REFERENCES

Beymer, L., Hill, J. C., & Osmon, W. (1987). *A study of the dropout situation in the state of Indiana.* Terre Haute, IN: School of Education, Indiana State University.

Cowley, T., & Ramo, J. (1993, July 26). The non-young and the restless. *Newsweek,* pp. 48–49.

Fordham, S. (1988). Racelessness as a factor in black students' school success: Pragmatic strategy or pyrric victory? *Harvard Educational Review, 58*(1), 54–84.

Fordham, S., & Ogbu, J. (1986). Black students' school success: Coping with the "burden of acting white." *The Urban Review, 18*(3), 176–206.

Grossman, H. (1991). Multicultural classroom management. *Contemporary Education, 62,* 161–165.

Harness, B. Z., Epstein, R., & Gordon, H. W. (1984). Cognitive profiles of children referred to a clinic for reading disabilities. *Journal of Learning Disabilities, 17,* 346–351.

Hetherington, E. M., Cox, M., & Cox, R. (1978). The aftermath of divorce. In J. H. Stevens, Jr., & M. Mathews (Eds.), *Mother-child, father-child relationships* (pp. 149–176). Washington, DC: National Association for the Education of Young Children.

Hier, D. B. (1979). Sex differences in hemisphere specialization: Hypothesis for the excess of dyslexia in boys. *Bulletin of the Orton Society, 29,* 74–83.

Krumboltz, J. D. (1988). The key to achievement: Learning to love learning. In G.R. Walz (Ed.), *Research and counseling: Building strong school counseling programs* (pp. 1–39). Alexandria, VA: American Association for Counseling and Development.

Lee, C. C. (1992). *Empowering young black males.* Ann Arbor, MI: ERIC Counseling and Personnel Services Clearinghouse.

Lefkowitz, B. (1987). *Tough change: Growing up on your own in America.* New York: The Free Press.

Miedzian, M. (1991). *Boys will be boys.* Garden City, NY: Doubleday.

Moir, A., & Jessel, D. (1991). *Brain sex. The real difference between men and women.* New York: Dell Publishing.

Pasteur, A. B., & Toldson, I. L. (1982). *Roots of soul: The psychology of Black expressiveness.* New York: Anchor.

Phipps, P. A. (1982). The LD learner is often a boy—Why? *Academic Therapy, 17,* 425–430.

Raspberry, W. (1990, August 28). The academic woes of black males. *The Indianapolis Star,* Op-Ed page.

Restak, R. M. (1979). *The brain: The last frontier.* New York: Warner Books.

Sadker, M., Sadker, D., & Donald, M. (1989). Subtle sexism in school. *Contemporary Education, 60*(4), 204–212.

Schumacher, D. (1992, February 17). Hispanics fair poorly in system many mistrust; Feel hobbled by stereotypes, school segregation. *Education USA,* pp. 145, 147.

Sexton, P. (1969). *The feminized male.* New York: Random House.

Tyler, L. E. (1965). *The psychology of human differences.* New York: Appleton-Century-Crofts.

CHAPTER 5

BOYS AND THEIR FAMILIES

To really understand behavior, observation of individuals in isolation from others is insufficient. Group settings for behavior are important, and the most primary of these is the family. It is no exaggeration to generalize that, if the family context for growth and behavior is functional and facilitating, boys are likely to evolve into manhood successfully. If or when it becomes dysfunctional, boy children are among the first casualties.

THE FAMILY

For many centuries, the word *family* referred to authority relationships, rather than emotional bonds between individuals. Even today the word is used in some criminal cultures to refer to a band of individuals disciplined by strong authority figures. Traditionally, we have come to think of *family* as a group of people living together, related by blood, marriage, or adoption. In recent times, the term refers to a group of people living together who love and care for each other—a definition based on relationships, rather than authority. Regardless of traditional or contemporary definition, the family context is the setting for the metamorphosis of young boys into young men.

Occasionally researchers come up with findings that provide unexpected insights on how important the family is to young boys. For example, research into the dynamics of the dual-career family discovered that boys are more likely to evidence lower academic achievement and psychological adjustment if both of their parents are employed outside the home (Bennett & Reardon, 1985). When presented video depictions of various forms of dual-career couples, young male adolescents responded more negatively (Malloy, 1991).

BOYS AND THEIR MOTHERS

Although it is the father who is responsible for the biological maleness of his child, it is usually the mother who provides his first environment. After his birth, she continues to serve as the primary caregiver, providing nourishment, comfort, and safety. The young boy first adjusts his behavior to this woman's world, but sooner or later he must renounce it, separate himself from it, and identify with what he perceives to be a man's world. If the father is present to share in child husbandry, it is easier for the little boy to switch identifications, and less need to repress his emotions.

Most mothers can specify the approximate date when their sweet little boy suddenly refused to be cuddled, kiss Aunt Mable goodbye, and stay clean and neat, and when he first used four-letter words. She usually explains this as a failure of her parenting; Freud explained it as the Oedipal complex. Nevertheless, mothers and sons have a very special relationship; nobody remembers having ever seen an athlete wave to a television camera and say, "Hi Dad!" Although in the eyes of his father he eventually becomes a man, in her eyes he is always her little boy. This has obvious advantages and disadvantages.

BOYS AND THEIR FATHERS

It is curious and surprising to note that, until about the middle of the 1970s, fathers were not studied very often in child development research investigations. Fathers were considered unimportant in the social and emotional development of their children, thus almost all studies focused on mothers (Boyd, 1985). This bias came from several sources. Many theories, such as Freudian theory and attachment theory, minimized fathers as major influencers of child behavior. Data were easier to collect from mothers because fathers were away working during the day. Sexist societal norms assumed that it was the duty of the father to be the economic provider, and that fathers do not spend much time with their children anyway. For all these reasons, it was fashionable to consider the mothering relationship as the crucial variable. "Mother bashing" was elevated to a high art by many who studied child misbehavior. Any and all imperfections in behavior were blamed upon what mothers did or did not do at the proper time in the proper manner.

In the past two decades, a plethora of studies have demonstrated that fathers can and do influence children in ways that are not that much different from mothers (Lamb, 1976). Fathers influence the development of children of both sexes, but are especially influential with their sons. Unfortunately, comparatively little research has been published on African-American fathers and their male offspring, so the following generalizations apply to White fathers and sons only.

1. Few fathers view themselves as practitioners of behavioral modification, but most of them utilize reward and punishment to shape child behavior.

2. The father's conduct serves as a model of masculinity, morality, and deportment. Boys often pattern their relationships with females after what they observe between their father and mother. It has been suggested that one of the best things fathers can do for their sons is to be good husbands.

3. Fathers teach skills that are important at that time and in the future. Sports, hobbies, social manners, use of tools, and literally hundreds of lessons are taught by fathers and learned by sons.

4. Fathers provide economic resources that acquire the basic necessities of life, such as food, housing, clothing, and medical care. Economic resources make it possible for sons to participate in a wide range of activities. Team sports require athletic equipment and transportation, music lessons require fees and an instrument, and television sets and home computers augment formal learning in school.

5. Positive father interest in academic performance is positively related to the boys' intellectual development, cognitive style, and academic success.

6. Boys who have warm relationships with their fathers tend to be better adjusted and more socially competent.

Fathers cannot make contributions to the growth and development of their sons if they are not participating in the family's day-to-day activities. If fathers are not present in the family to make the contributions to their sons' development (listed previously), then two consequences are possible: either the boys will find some substitute source, or that aspect of the boys' development will be underdeveloped, distorted, or stunted. Fathers become absent because of long-term military duty, death, or divorce. Damage can also occur in those instances where fathers are so intensively engrossed in their careers that they cancel out their physical presence with their psychological absence. Boys without fathers in the family are at risk for increased delinquency, sex-role confusion, and problems in academic performance (Hamilton, 1977). It is very difficult for boys to act like men if their fathers are off someplace acting like boys.

THE DEVASTATION OF DIVORCE

Currently, about one half of all first marriages end up in divorce, and 60% of second marriages also fail. Each day the parents of at least 2,750 children separate or divorce. In 1990, a record 407,000 minors were placed in foster homes—up 66% since 1983 (Richman, 1992). The majority (57%) of people who get divorced have children under age 18 (Magnet, 1992). *Fortune* magazine estimated that the parents of approximately 2,750 children separate or divorce each day, and that more than half of all White boys and three quarters of all African-American boys under 18 will spend part of their childhoods in single-parent households (Richman, 1992). It has been estimated that about one child in four now lives in a single-parent family, and that number is expected to grow.

The divorce rate is considerably higher for African-American children. Fewer African Americans marry, and they are more than twice as likely as Whites to separate or divorce. In about 60% of African-American families with children, there is only one parent, compared with about 20% of such White families (Otten, 1986).

Of children who live with their biological mothers, more than one third have no contact with their biological fathers (Seltzer & Bianchi, 1988). A National Survey of Children study indicated that only one child in six sees his or her father as often as once a week; almost one half did not see him at all in the past year (Whitehead, 1993).

DEBATE AND DISAGREEMENT ON EFFECTS

Coontz (1992) discounted the negative effects of divorce on children in three arguments. Her thesis is that there were no "good old days" of the family, and that today's situation is not all that bad by comparison. She cited evidence comparing children in single-parent families with those in two-parent families where there is conflict and divorce, and concluded that children from quarreling intact families are "no better off" than children of divorced parents. It would appear to be more useful to make functional families the comparison group.

Coontz pointed out that many of the behavioral disorders of boys after divorce were also there before divorce. However, a longitudinal study comparing boys whose families went through divorce with those that remained intact showed that about one half of what appear to be the negative effects of divorce started during the early stages of conflict and family stress before actual separation and divorce (Cherlin et al., 1991). It is not the legal formality of divorce, but the emotional environment that triggers the problems.

Her third argument is that kids today spend about as much time with parents as did children of Colonial times, when marriages averaged only about 12 years because of high mortality rates of mothers in pregnancy and childbirth and fathers in work accidents and disease. Bettelheim (1976) observed that, in Colonial America, the average age of a child on losing a parent was 14. This perception may be accurate, but it is irrelevant. The difference is that, at that time in America, most boys had left their homes by age 12 or so to enter the labor force. Today boys are kept economically, educationally, and emotionally dependent on parent or parents well into their third decade of life. In addition, the effects of the loss of a parent have always been less damaging for a mid-teenager than for a young boy. For example, Parke (1981) reported that if the father leaves before his son is 6 years old, the boy will be more dependent on peers and less assertive.

Equating the loss of a parent by death with the loss of a parent through divorce seems unjustified. It is ironic that family survivors appear to recover quicker and to be better off economically and psychologically when a parent is lost to the family by death rather than by divorce. Society is more sympathetic, understanding, supportive, and generous with resources if a child loses a parent via premature death rather than through divorce or abandonment.

Claims discounting the negative effects of divorce on children have a hollow ring—often a mixture of guilt and lame rationalizations:

"Our shortened time together is quality time."

"Most married parents don't spend much time with their kids, either."

"They'll get over it."

In the Persian Gulf War, Pentagon press agents concocted a new title for the innocent bystanders severely injured in warfare: *collateral damage*. This term fits the children of divorced adults. Elementary school counselors know this; secondary school counselors may be less aware because at that age and stage feelings are not always expressed directly. This situation is presented poignantly in a little volume containing 110 quotations from children ages 7–18 on how they were affected and learned how to cope with their parents' divorce (Spauge, 1992).

THE EVIDENCE

Literally hundreds of studies on the effects of divorce on children's behavior have been published in the last 25 years. The consensus generalizations are: (a) that children of divorce exhibit more social, academic, and personal adjustment problems than do peers from intact families; (b) that separation of their parents is stressful for all and traumatic for many; (c) and that the effects differ for boys. Contrary to popular belief and the rationalizations of divorced parents, children do not "bounce back" after the trauma of the their parents' divorce. The damage often persists far into adulthood.

The first noticeable effect of divorce is typically a sharp decline in standard of living, especially when the mother has custody. To be a single mother is to be poor. After divorce, the mother has to "make do" with an average annual income of $13,500 if she is White and $9,000 if she is non-White. At the same time, the White nonresident father has an average income of $25,000, and the non-White father $13,600. One estimate is that the mother–children income drops an average of 30% (Whitehead, 1993). In 1991, 16 million children in 10 million households were living without a father, half of whom were not paying all the child support they owed and a fourth paying nothing at all. A quarter of those families were living below the poverty level (Hall, 1991). Children in single-parent families typically have less than a third of the median per capita income of peers from two-parent families, half falling below the poverty line after divorce (Magnet, 1992).

The restricted budget has little room for a boy's trendy sneakers, fashionable clothes, or orthodontia, and his own used car is out of the question. Other more subtle effects are worse. This sharp decline in standard of living triggers a domino effect. About 38% of divorced mothers and their dependent children are forced to change residences and move to cheaper housing the first year after the divorce (Whitehead, 1993). Thus, the boy who has just lost his father is often ripped away from his school, friends, and teammates. If the mother now has to work, or work more, he also loses her presence and attention. Within a short period of time, he can lose nearly all of his social and emotional relationships.

In our society, it is very difficult to construct psychological security on the shifting sands of economic instability. The divorce of parents adversely affects the behavior of their children in a sharply negative direction. Hetherington, Cox, and Cox (1978) reported that divorced parents make (a) fewer maturity demands on their children, (b) are less affectionate, and (c) exhibit marked inconsistency in matters of discipline and control. Sons are affected this way more often (Bronfenbrenner, 1984).

Boys are less likely to heed their mother's directions, but more likely to comply with their father's, if and when he comes around. Frequently the divorced mother transfers her hostility toward the absent father to the son, whom she sees as his image. Satir (1972) wrote that "Boys in a one-parent family probably face the greatest trap—being over-mothered, and/or getting the picture that the female was the dominant one in society, ending up with feeling that the male is nothing" (p. 172).

The newly divorced mother must attend to her job, manage the household, and begin constructing a new life for herself while being stalked by demanding children. Soon the boy senses that he has lost a father, as well as the attention of his mother. If she goes to work full time, the son is typically resentful (Bronfenbrenner, 1985).

As their separated biological parents form new relationships, boys are assaulted by waves of emotional conflicts. Because 80% of divorced fathers remarry (Whitehead, 1993), their already divided attention to their sons is further subdivided toward their new wives and perhaps step children. Many boys deeply resent their mother's new male friendships; if one eventually results in a stepfather, family fireworks are a distinct possibility.

Behavior at school deteriorates. Boys from divorced families are more disruptive and aggressive in the classroom, less likely to complete school assignments, and less likely to be prepared and attentive in class. Anxiety, physical aggression, and difficulties in concentration are easily identified. In one study of elementary school students, having a father with the same last name in the household significantly reduced the likelihood that a student would be a candidate for psychological services (Harvey, 1979). Fears, anger, and frustrations accompany them to school and are unloaded on a wide variety of innocent bystanders, who understandably do not feel that they deserve the transferred hostility and aggression.

Academic performance is also adversely affected by divorce. A National Association of Elementary School Principals study showed that 33% of two-parent elementary school children were ranked as high achievers, compared with only 17% of single-parent students. Emotional incapacitation overwhelms intellectual capacity. Teachers report that such students do not pay attention and do not concentrate on tasks. Their minds seem to be distracted elsewhere, often to the stressful situation at home. Boys from divorced families score lower on reading and math tests; are absent more often; are more anxious, hostile, and withdrawn; and are less popular with their peers. They are twice as likely to drop out of high school.

Their wounds are long lasting: Years later, such boys find it more difficult to form their own intimate, loving relationships (Magnet, 1992). Fathering is a learned response; if you never had a good teacher, how are you supposed to learn how to play the role yourself? Kaye (1989) conducted a longitudinal study of 234 children from divorced families and 223 children from intact families. Five years later, the boys from broken families exhibited both lower achievement test scores and course grades. Five years after divorce, more than a third of children of divorce were found to be suffering from moderate or severe depression (Wallerstein & Blakeslee, 1989). Feelings of confusion, rejection, anger, and suffering last a long time. Many adult men continue to grieve about the divorce of their parents and the loss of the family environment they once enjoyed. The secret of raising a boy is not apparent. It is two parents. Anything less is considerable less.

IMPLICATIONS FOR COUNSELORS

Relatively few school counselors have the time, training, or mandate to engage in marriage and family therapy with students and their parents. Nevertheless, there are many things that they can do to ease the situations.

Be alert to sudden changes in academic performance or interpersonal behavior with peers or teachers. Like a canary in a coal mine, boys seem to have an early warning system of family disintegration. Boys are sensitive to parental conflicts, and typically begin exhibiting dysfunctional behavior long before the actual fracture of the family.

Sometimes a boy engages in highly visible behavior in a subconscious attempt to draw his parents' attention away from each other and their differences and to him and his problems. If he does not have any problems at the moment, he will create some. Sometimes this takes the form of deliberate disciplinary violations. He may commit "academic suicide," suddenly failing subjects he usually masters with ease.

When the boy misbehaves, fails, or rebels at school, it is natural for parents to assume that he has the problem. Parents seldom consider themselves to be the problem, or even a part of the problem. Working with the boy under these circumstances is tricky; if he communicates the insight he gains through counseling to his parents, they are not likely to express appreciation to the school counselor.

Role reversal is not uncommon. It is ironic that even small children often function in such a manner as to parent their parents. Children are encouraged to be sympathetic, understanding, and comforting to their poor unhappy mother and father. Even small children have been observed mothering their mothers. The following example comes from a recently divorced mother.

> After Tom left, my self-confidence plummeted as I realized all the things he did that I now had to do, but didn't know how to do. He paid the bills, planned the vacations, and always drove the car on trips. The first time I drove in a big city, I was a nervous wreck. At that time, Kevin was about 9. I thought I was doing a good job and not showing now nervous I was, but on the way home he took my hand and told me that I had done a good job. It is amazing what kids can detect.

Boys can become entangled in the war between the parents, who are quick to use him as an ally, rather than an innocent bystander and victim. He may be pressured to take sides with one parent against the other. He may be blamed for causing the problem. Sensitive boys are apt to become symptom bearers. In some cases, the oldest boy begins to assume the male head of the family role. In any event, his role and behavior as a maturing adolescent male is interrupted and distorted.

Some boys learn how to play one guilty parent against the other to get what they want. They seem to feel justified in returning some of the pain they feel.

Outbursts should not be taken personally. Sometimes the boy transfers his anger and aggression at school on a scapegoat. He may be reacting in a way at school that he cannot do at home. This does not mean that educators should be tolerant of all conduct, but it does suggest that placing behaviors in context might make them more understandable.

Several kinds of families will be encountered. The deficit family is restricted on the psychological and economic contributions that can go to sons. In the dysfunctional family, the children can be mentally healthy, the parents not. Sometimes the boy is the most mentally healthy and mature person in the family. Often his behavior is actually normal, and not to be unexpected under the circumstances he is experiencing.

It is not always easy to find ways to share insights with others who have part of the responsibility for the boy's welfare. Many times the behaviors that teachers find unjustified and puzzling would make sense to them if they knew and understood the family context. However, confidentiality severely limits the information that can be shared. Consider the following examples.

> Teachers complain that Earl no longer turns in his homework. Earl tells the counselor that several evenings a week while his mother is at her job his stepfather makes him leave the house for a couple of hours so he can invite his lady friend in for a visit. He threatens to beat Earl if he tells his mother what's going on.

> Donnie is wild during the first period, moving about the room, talking constantly, and burning energy. The counselor learns that he lives in a small trailer at the edge of town with his mother, his mother's boyfriend of the week, his grandmother, a younger sister and brother, and a cat. In winter, this becomes an aluminum pressure cooker, with noise, smells, no privacy, and certainly no place to do homework. By the time he gets to school, he is ready to explode.

> Duane demonstrates average academic motivation and ability, but his father insists that he be placed in advanced aca-

demic classes. Teachers protest that this will result in massive academic frustration and failure.

Leon is more than "intellectually challenged"—he is severely mentally handicapped. His socially prominent parents display a public attitude of solicitous concern about his academic welfare. In conference with the counselor, they display their true feelings of shame, embarrassment, and rejection. The counselor suspects that Leon knows how his parents feel.

The coaching staff continues the tradition of a father–son banquet even though more than a third of the team members have neither a father nor a stepfather. Rather than showing up alone, most of them refuse to attend. The coaches take the position that, if you are not present, you cannot receive your team award.

Counselors must constantly strive to develop a relationship of trust with teachers and administrators at a level where they will accept advice and recommendations without becoming privy to all the actual details of situations. Most teachers are ready and willing to work out alternative arrangements if they are taken into limited confidence, and believe that the boy finds himself in a situation where he deserves some temporary special consideration.

Make time in the guidance program for group counseling. Counselors may have to seek out boys and persuade them to participate, but the benefits can be substantial. Being fatherless is not a problem with a solution, but boys can learn how to manage situations more satisfactorily.

Boys also need to become involved in parent-education programs far in advance of assuming the real responsibility. Pittman (1991) concluded that "It is hard to imagine how we can raise a better generation of sons until we have a better generation of fathers." Breaking the cycle mandates starting somewhere; perhaps the period of early adolescence will prove to be the most efficient and effective place to begin.

With situational management as a goal, counselors can help the members of the group to work through the stages of sadness, guilt, anger, acceptance, and forgiveness. The fact that different members of the group are likely to be at different stages is actually helpful in illustrating two facts: (a) nobody is all alone in experiencing this trauma, and (b) it is possible to salvage the best from an unfortunate situation.

It is remotely possible that we would have a better society if every youngster had a high school course in physics. It is probable that we would have a better society if every youngster had a course in parenting, a learnable skill. Boys can come to understand, manage, and perhaps overcome their fathering problems, and learn how not to repeat the sad circle when they have a boy to raise.

Become involved in efforts to move against problems while they are small and at least possibly manageable. The U.S. Department of Health and Human Services and the U.S. Department of Education have recently cooperated in publishing a 157-page book of practical policies, procedures, and programs. Entitled "Together We Can: A Guide for Crafting a Profamily System of Education and Human Services," it is a practical guide that features a holistic approach to ministering to the problems of children and their families (Melaville, Blank, & Asayesh, 1993).

Know, accept, and acknowledge your level of training before becoming involved with family members other than the student. Few school counselors have the time, training, or mandate to engage in marriage and family therapy. Referral to someone with more training and experience with a situation is not a sign of weakness—it is a duty of all professionals.

In summary, the family is the first and most influential learning environment. Boys spend more of their lives with "them" than with "us." Lessons learned in the family, and lessons not learned there, are powerful determinants of the behaviors expected in the school, on the street, and in life.

The importance of family contributions to identity and behavior is demonstrated by the fact that, often when the traditional family breaks down and becomes dysfunctional, many boys gravitate toward artificial families (e.g., gangs), which appear to offer the identity, status, structure, and safety otherwise lacking in their lives.

Family therapists contend that behavior can only be understood in context—an enormous challenge to the school counselor who often does not have enough time to interact with all students, let alone their families. Nevertheless, if the school, the boy, and his family can find ways to work together consistently toward mutually shared goals, the chances of bringing about meaningful differences in his life can be dramatically improved.

REFERENCES

Bennett, B., & Reardon, R. (1985). Dual-career couples and the psychological adjustment of offspring: A review. *The School Counselor, 32*, 287–295.

Bettelheim, B. (1976, September/October). Untying the family. *The Center Magazine*, pp. 5–9.

Boyd, S. T. (1985). Study of the father: Research methods. *American Behavioral Scientist, 29*, 112–128.

Bronfenbrenner, U. (1985). The parent/child relationship in our changing society. In L. Eugene Arnold (Ed.), *Parents, children, and change* (pp. 45–57). Lexington, MA: Lexington/Heath Books.

Cherlin, A. J., Furstenberg, F. F., Lindsay Chase-Lansdale, P., Kiernan, K., Robins, P. K., Morrison, D. R., & Teitler, J. O. (1991). Longitudinal studies of effects of divorce on children in Great Britain and the United States. *Science, 252*, 1386–1389.

Coontz, S. (1992). *The way we never were.* New York: Basic Books.

Hall, M. (1991, October 11). Census report: 16 million kids live without dad. *USA Today*, p. 6A.

Hamilton, M. L. (1977). *Father's influence on children.* Chicago: Nelson-Hall.

Harvey, V. G. S. (1979). *The effect of relative age and other variables on rate of referral for school psychological services.* Unpublished doctoral dissertation, Indiana University, Bloomington, IN.

Hetherington, E., Cox, R., & Cox, R. (1978). The aftermath of divorce. In J.H. Stevens, Jr., & M. Mathews (Eds.), *Mother–child relations.* Washington, DC: National Association for the Education of Young Children.

Kaye, S. H. (1989). The impact of divorce on children's academic performance. *Children of divorce: Developmental and clinical issues.* Binghamton, NY: Haworth.

Lamb, M. E. (Ed.). (1976). *The role of the father in child development.* New York: Wiley.

Magnet, M. (1992, August 10). The American family, 1992. *Fortune*, pp. 42–47.

Malloy, L. (1991). *Young adolescents' attitudes toward occupational sex-typing and dual-career couples.* Unpublished doctoral dissertation, Indiana State University, Terre Haute, IN.

Melaville, A., Blank, M., & Asayesh, G. (1993). *Together we can: A guide for crafting a profamily system of education and human services.* Washington, DC: U.S. Department of Educational Research and Human Improvement, U.S. Department of Health and Human Services.

Otten, A. L. (1986, September 26). Deceptive picture: If you see families staging a comeback it's probably a mirage. *The Wall Street Journal*, pp. 1, 19.

Parke, R. D. (1981). *Father.* Cambridge, MA: Harvard University Press.

Pittman, F. (1991, May/June). The masculine mystique. *The Family Therapy Networker, 14,* pp. 40–52.

Richman, L. S. (1992, August 10). Struggling to save our kids. *Fortune,* pp. 34–40.

Satir, V. (1972). *People-making.* Palo Alto, CA: Science and Behavior Books.

Seltzer, J. A., & Bianchi, S. M. (1988). Children's contact with absent parents. *Journal of Marriage and the Family, 50,* 663–677.

Spauge, G. (Ed.). (1992). *My parents got a divorce.* Elgin, IL: David C. Cook Publishing Co.

Wallerstein, J., & Blakeslee, S. (1989). *Second chances: Men, women, and children a decade after divorce.* New York: Tichnor & Fields.

Whitehead, B. D. (1993, April). Dan Quayle was right. *Atlantic Monthly, 271,* pp. 47–84.

CHAPTER 6

SOCIAL GROUPINGS:
FRIENDS, PEERS, AND GANGS

Interactions and relationships with others outside the family circle are important parts of the life of young males. Male friends are the first extrafamily relationships of most boys, and friends made before the age of 20 frequently persist throughout life. When family and normal peer groups fail, resourceful males invent artificial structures called *gangs*—a social structure seldom beneficial.

BOYS' FRIENDSHIP PATTERNS

From a developmental point of view, boys' friendship patterns can be divided into four phases: childhood, juvenile, preadolescent, and adolescent. Not all activities pursued in a group result in friendships. Childhood parallel play refers to activities performed in the presence of others, but not involving them. By age 2 or 3, most boys seem to recognize other familiar boys from whom they expect predictable responses and with whom they engage in enjoyable activities (Rubin, 1980). Soon afterward, exclusion as well as inclusion of playmates can be observed.

By age 3, it becomes obvious that children prefer and seek out same-sex friendships and playmates. According to Rubin (1980), by about the sixth grade, the sex separation of friendship groups is almost total. Between the ages of 6 and 9, juvenile boys begin interacting within peer groups, rather than with one other boy. Because these groups are usually formed in the neighborhood, they are quite homogeneous in age, socioeconomic class, and intelligence. Their time together is spent riding bikes, playing games, participating in team sports, and fantasy/pretending activities such as "playing war." In general, when boys get together they *do* things together, rather than engage in talk about themselves or their activities. Through such group activities, they find validation of themselves through what they *do* rather than what they *discuss*. They express little or any interest in where the girls are or what they are doing. One of the harsh realities of group behavior at this stage is the cruel way that such groups often practice exclusion. Denying participative membership to one who wants to be a part of the group can be devastating.

Sullivan (1953) marked the end of the juvenile era and the beginning of the preadolescence phase at the point where the boy establishes a best-friend relationship with a boy of the same age—a "chum." A close friend is the first step toward autonomy from family. The adolescent peer group begins to take its place as an alternative to the family group, which soon falls to at least second in importance as a reference group and sounding board. What the friend or the group thinks seems to prevail, much to the consternation of many parents. The interaction between such special friends is thought to be important in the forging of feelings of self-worth, interpersonal sensitivity, and other social attributes thought to be important.

Since the first data on adolescents in this culture were collected, it has been demonstrated that boys need close companions with whom to share their problems, which usually include developmental predicaments involving parents, school, changing bodies, emerging sexuality, and the future. Through the process of explaining their problems and feelings to another person, they explain them to themselves. The youngster lucky enough to have a friend who accepts him as he is without criticism, who listens carefully, and refrains from criticism is lucky indeed. (Note how the characteristics of an ideal best friend resemble those of the effective person-centered counselor.)

With the onset of adolescence, the first signs of cross-sex friendships appear, although same-sex friendship cliques continue to predominate. The cross-sex interest and the first experiences for boys seem to begin about the ninth grade, 2 years later than for girls. Male participation in cross-sex groups increases. At this time, the relationship to females is not romantic in nature, although that season will soon arrive. To be chosen by another person as a special friend is an important boost to self-esteem—a special signal to self and observing others.

Up to this stage, boys typically have not divulged many of their private feelings to anybody, not even to their closest male friend. Now many begin to look to cross-sex relationships for emotional gratification—sharing aspects of their lives and concerns that are not disclosed to anybody else with a female peer.

IMPLICATIONS FOR COUNSELORS

Understanding the evolving relationship of the individual boy to his peer groups can often bring meaning to otherwise puzzling behavior. Teachers and counselors know that boys exhibit different behaviors individually in private than they do in public where others are watching. Confrontations can be avoided by not calling for public behaviors that force boys to choose between peer and adult approval. In such a dilemma, they are likely to choose group norms, rather than those they might privately prefer.

Insightful school counselors can relate to young males in a non-threatening manner. Counselors who play the parent role with their male clients should not be surprised when their clients relate to them like they do to their real parents. Who needs another critical, punitive, preachy parent figure in their life in times like these?

Losing a friend can be a blow, whether that loss be by death, moving to another school, or a rupture of the friendship bond for logical or illogical reasons. Until the boy has a background of experience to handle such losses, the counselor may have to provide appropriate understanding, perspectives, and optimism.

Consider the motivations and the possible consequences of any recommended actions to meddle with what appears to be normal same-sex and cross-sex development. Attempts to force acceleration of cross-sex interactions are unwise. The more-mature young females and relevant adults need to have patience with young males; eventually they will evolve from little boys into young men. Attempts to accelerate the natural process may produce unintended negative results. Back off and enjoy them as they are, knowing that what you see will not last long.

WHEN FRIENDSHIP GROUPS BECOME GANGS

Adults have always been fascinated, entertained, and sometimes threatened by the behavior of young males in organized groups. *The Blackboard Jungle*, depicting high school punks hazing a dedicated teacher, was a hit movie in 1955. *Romeo and Juliet* was given a contemporary New York City gang warfare context, a score by Leonard Bernstein and Stephen Sondheim, and became the Broadway and movie masterpiece *West Side Story*. Charles Dickens' tale of boy thieves of London was romanticized and expanded into the smash hit Broadway musical and movie Oscar winner, *Oliver*. In recent years, we have been presented with more starkly realistic and frightening movies on gang behaviors in such movies as *Colors*, *Boyz 'n the Hood*, *New Jack City*, and *Juice*. For many citizens today, contemporary depictions of gang behavior are neither amusing nor entertaining.

Young males organize themselves into groups and affiliate with existing groups many times on their journey to adulthood. Sports teams, 4-H clubs, Boy Scouts, and fraternities come to mind as examples. These organizations are characterized by colors, names, symbols, rituals, and internal rules and sanctions designed to mold conforming behaviors.

Boys join gangs for many of the same reasons anybody affiliates with any organization: camaraderie, a need to belong to something, protection and power through numbers, the comfort of operating within specified rules and structure, association with others who give you some attention and care about you as an individual, a setting for making new friends and contacts, and the enjoyment, pleasure, and satisfaction from sharing experiences with others similar to yourself. The exaggerated need for respect is paramount; to be disrespected, or "dissed," no matter how trivial the assumed insult may be, is sufficient cause for confrontation and retaliation.

As one teacher in Los Angeles commented to the author, "In this neighborhood we call them gangs, a few blocks south of here groups of young males the same age and organized for many of the same reasons are called fraternities." The big difference is that members of fraternities do not kill members of other fraternities. At least not very often. Unfortunately, many gang members do. Often.

DEFINITION GENERALITIES

To law-enforcement officials, the umbrella term *gang* is applied to groups that are organized to practice unlawful activities. Otherwise, they would be a club or a team. The following are gang characteristics:

1. A gang is a group whose members form an alliance for a common purpose or purposes through unlawful behavior and violence if necessary.
2. Gangs may have strong centralized leadership and internal organization, or be a loosely knit assembly.
3. All gangs have strict codes of conduct for their members, with stern sanctions for deviations. Gang rules supersede family rules, school rules, and community rules.
4. A common goal is to engage in activities that are intended to result in respect and deference by others. The reputation of a gang is more important than any of its members.
5. Gang leadership is often effective; not only are they "streetwise," but they understand the art of manipulation and intimidation.
6. Coed gangs are rare. Females associated with male gangs are there for utilitarian purposes: (a) for sex, and (b) as a safe place to stash contraband when the police, who are usually reluctant to search females, show up.
7. Gangs usually form along ethnic or racial lines, but regional exceptions exist.
8. Gangs are not restricted to major metropolitan areas or among low socioeconomic populations.
9. Pregang behavior usually begins in elementary school, is in place by the junior high school years, and is most active among late teens and early twenties.
10. Violence seems unfortunately inevitable. Once a boy becomes a gang member, it is inevitable that he will become either a victim or a perpetrator of violence, or both. About 85% of juvenile offenses are committed in groups of two or more (Ingrassia, Annin, Biddle, & Miller, 1993).

Activities

Many of the activities of gangs and individual gang members have consequences that impact negatively on community and school environments.

Communication. Gangs communicate through colors, grooming, fashions, symbols, and language. They are proud of their affiliations, and dress and behave in such a way as to make this clear to all observers. The youth gangs of today are not secret societies.

In many schools across the nation, it is traditional to encourage all students to wear the school colors on the day of the big game.

Gangs have adopted the same idea, and typically choose some day of the week to advertise their affiliations. In one midwestern metropolitan school system, Friday is "color day" for the gangs—"fighting and brawling day" to school officials. Some gangs have adopted professional sports team clothing, wearing baseball caps backward or at an angle. Bandannas or "rags" may be worn hanging out a rear pocket, as a headband, or simply draped over a jacket. The purpose is to communicate membership to both friend and foe. Baggy shirts and jackets make it easier to conceal weapons. Shoes are important signals, by style, brand, or color of shoe, or the shoe laces, which may not be the same colors.

Hairstyle is a highly visible signal. Sometimes names or symbols are cut out down to the scalp. Common styles include longer and shorter hair on parts of the head, braids, shaved or cropped hair, or distinctive designs.

Many gang members display tattoos, sometimes self-inflicted, to identify their affiliation. Younger members frequently write on their fingers or arms with indelible pens. Asian gangs use tattoos frequently, with eagles indicating Vietnamese gang membership. Filipino gang members often burn themselves with cigarettes on arms and chest, with more scars indicating longer membership or higher rank. Dark glasses are popular with Hispanic gang members, some of whom wear them day and night (Students At Risk Resource Network, 1991).

Defending a Territory. Wild animals mark the boundaries of their territory and savagely attack intruders. Suburban real estate homeowners' associations organize to defend real estate they do not yet completely own. Gangs defend real estate they will never own. It is relatively easy to color a map to show areas of dominant gang influence.

Gangs stake out their claimed turf and mark its boundaries with distinctive graffiti logos or symbols. At one time, law-enforcement officials maintained records of cattle brands; now they publish guides to gang trademark graffiti.

Nicknames Are Part of the Process. Members are typically known within gangs by nicknames assigned by veteran members. As with gang logos, law-enforcement officials maintain computer cross-files in order to trace individuals by their real and gang "monikers." Most gang members do not know the legal names of all the other members of their organization.

Violence Is a Way of Life. Initiation into a gang often involves violence. Sometimes the initiate has to beat up a member of a rival group, break into residences, or perhaps cut or shoot some rival. He may be forced to take blows from gang members to demonstrate his obedience and toughness. Gangs seek out confrontations with rival groups—violence that claims a heavy toll on intended and innocent victims. It is ironic that gang members' violence is discharged against members of other gangs that look like themselves—their mirror images. Psychodynamic interpretations suggest that, in killing or harming "him," they are in fact striking out at themselves.

Vandalism and Defacing of Public and Private Property. Many of the graffiti "artworks" are the product of innocent-looking, middle-class, bored suburban White boys with pockets full of aerosol paint cans. Roving graffiti bands deface walls, traffic signs, mass transportation vehicles, overpasses, and any other reachable surface by placing their signatures, called *tags*, for any and all to see. Seeking instant fame, they often risk life and limb to deface almost inaccessible surfaces. If and when rival bands of taggers deface another's work, violence may follow.

Unlawful, Illegal Behaviors. We are not dealing with an Oliver Twist world of the wiley Fagin's band of mischievous juvenile pickpockets. Today's criminal gang activities typically include selling and using drugs, theft, burglary, illegal weapons, larceny, robbery, extortion, assault and battery, vandalism, arson, and murder. Concentrated gang activity endangers innocent bystanders, drives away customers, increases insurance costs, and eventually forces businesses to fail and flee the gang war zone. American youth gangs in the 1990s are a serious challenge to law and order, public safety, and the kind of society we will have at the turn of the century.

IMPLICATIONS FOR COUNSELORS

Gang activity is another predicament that counselors must try to manage, not a problem that they can solve. The school cannot remediate or reverse the effects of the failures, neglect, and collapse of responsibility by governmental, church, community, and social agencies and institutions.

Although gang-related activities and incidents do occur in school, the main arena for such activities is in the streets and community.

School officials can and should cooperate with community agencies and law enforcement, but off-campus gang monitoring, supervision, and control is not primarily a school issue.

Schools must accelerate efforts to find and implement ways to help all boys develop self-esteem and respect for self and others. The boy who lacks self-esteem-building experiences at home or in school may seek it on the streets by gangs, which offer well-defined norms and goals and a structural support system for transition into manhood. In the absence of the traditional family structure, almost anything else will do. Raphael (1989) concluded that "When a group—any group—offers a well-defined set of norms and goals, along with a method for living up to those norms and meeting those goals, we are given at least a semblance of structural support for our transition into manhood" (p. 110).

Counselors can join faculty teams to devise classroom-management strategies and cooperative-learning experiences that have the potential of reaching and including a wide spectrum of participation and potential for success. Students can be delegated real power to make real decisions in matters that are real and important to them. Such activities must begin in the elementary school and become a permanent component of secondary school education.

Establish and maintain close communication and liaison with law-enforcement and welfare professionals. Working together can generate cooperative actions that can be more successful than going it alone.

An early alert system to identify future gang members should be in place no later than late elementary or early junior high. These "wannabees" are frequently more volatile and dangerous than full-fledged gang members. They not only lack discipline, but often strive to do something spectacular to earn invitation to full gang membership.

Backover (1992) cited Capuzzi's description of those young boys who are at risk for future gang membership: (a) outsiders, (b) not involved in classroom activities, (c) difficulty communicating with adults, (d) low self-esteem, and (e) poor decision-making and problem-solving skills. All of these deficits are remediable and correctable by experiences the school can provide.

Be cautious about making generalizations about individuals who are gang members. In many settings, it is safer and more normal to join up with a gang than to go it alone. Counselors who know gang members as individuals have learned that many of them are reluctant warriors, still reachable and certainly still salvageable.

In Boston, a movement involving former gang members and college youths demonstrates one constructive way in which such energies can be diverted to constructive causes. Volunteers in the privately funded "City Year" project receive a weekly salary of $100, plus a $5,000 grant at the end of a 9-month work year. During that time, they register to vote, produce a resume, complete a tax-preparation workshop, and, if not high school graduates, study for the General Education Development (GED) exam. They work in schools, housing projects, parks, and other institutions that need help, but lack funds for full-time employees. One month is spent in an internship related to their career interests. This program may become a model for future government-supported national service opportunities.

In summary, if a boy is to think of himself as a man, he must live up to the perceptions of himself and those he thinks are important. If he is denied a good job, a decent place to live, something to hope and strive for, and something to protect from loss; if all the options open to others are closed to him, then we should not be surprised if he feels justified in seeking outlets and satisfactions in ways the majority of society defines as inappropriate. Boys who once worked and saved for a baseball glove now shop for guns in a deadly battle against fear and boredom.

Siegel (1973) wrote that every society is only 20 years away from barbarism because we have only that much time to teach the understanding, values, beliefs, and skills that make civilization, as we know it, possible. The fact that this is not being accomplished with a sizable minority of today's young males should be a matter of considerable concern.

REFERENCES

Backover, A. (1992). *Mean streets: The fatal attraction of youth gangs.* Alexandria, VA: American Counselor Association.

Ingrassia, M., Annin, P., Biddle, N., & Miller, S. (1993, July 19). Life means nothing. *Newsweek*, pp. 16–17.

Raphael, R. (1989). *The men from the boys: Rites of passage in male America.* Lincoln, NE: The University of Nebraska Press.

Rawlins, W. K. (1992). *Friendship matters.* New York: Walter de Gruyter.

Rubin, Z. (1980). *Children's friendships.* Cambridge, MA: Harvard University Press.

Siegel, A. (1973, October). *Stanford Observer.*

Students At Risk Resource Network. (1991). *Streetwise: A community information packet relating to gangs and drugs.* Oakland, CA: Schools-Community Partnership Anti-Gang/Drug Program.

Sullivan, H. S. (1953). *The interpersonal theory of psychiatry.* New York: Norton.

CHAPTER 7

WORKING FOR MONEY

One of our cherished national beliefs is the Protestant work ethic: Having a job and working develops personal qualities that lead to individual and national economic and spiritual success. This traditional work ethic has been comprehensively defined as follows:

> All honest work possesses innate dignity and worth. Excellence can be attained and is rewarded in any occupation. One should strive to do his best in whatever work he does. The worker who is satisfied with doing less than his best is, to some extent, dissatisfied with elf. The contributions one can make to society stem, to a large extent, from the work one does. Work is seen as possessing personal as well as financial rewards for the worker and the saying "A task well done is its own reward" has real meaning. Persons to whom the work is personally meaningful want to work, prepare themselves for work, and actively seek to work; they are, most of the time, happier when they are working than when they are not. A significant portion of the pride individuals have in themselves is seen as the best and surest route to the highest level of occupational success possible for the individual. (Hoyt, Evans, Mocklin, & Mangum, 1972, p. 101)

This standard has been applied to adults, as well as to children. Today an increasing accumulation of evidence suggests that this traditional work ethic is undergoing a radical transformation. Teenagers at work in today's economy and social matrix constitute a complex cluster of behaviors that is producing mixed results.

THE EXTENT OF TEENAGE EMPLOYMENT

For most youngsters, working for money starts early. The National Education Longitudinal Study surveyed nearly 25,000 eighth graders and found that four fifths of them reported working after school and during summers for pay. Baby-sitting, lawn mowing, table waiting, odd jobs, farm/manual labor, and clerk/sales office work were mentioned (U.S. Department of Education, 1991).

A General Accounting Office (GAO; 1991) study showed that 28% of all 15-year-olds and 51% of all 16- to 17-year-olds worked during 1988. Most were employed in retail trade (48%) and personal, professional, and repair services (25%). Low-income youths and minorities were less likely to be employed. One explanation for this is that the available jobs are in the suburban strip malls, and they live miles away with no adequate transportation. More children from low-income families worked in dangerous and hazardous work settings.

The National Education Association (NEA) published an estimate of the number of children ages 12-17 working today at 5.5 million, plus more than 600,000 12- and 13-year-olds (Trends, 1993). *Newsweek* magazine also placed the estimate at more than 5 million workers between the ages of 12 and 17 (Waldman & Springen, 1992).

CHILD LABOR LAWS

The use and the exploitation of children in the workplace, like violence, is as American as apple pie. For example, in 1900, 120,000 children were employed in Pennsylvania factories and coal mines, most of them starting by age 11. Most of the young miners died by age 30 because of accidents or black lung disease. In the early 1900s, children made up 23.7% of the workers in southern textile mills, with 12-hour shifts for children as young as 6 and 7. By 1920, half the workers in factories were boys and girls under age 11 (Coontz, 1992). Mason (1976) quoted a poem of that time by the reformer Sarah Cleghorn:

> The golf links lie so near the mill
> That almost every day
> The laboring children can look out
> And see the men at play.

American businessmen have traditionally resisted child labor laws. Early in this century, compulsory education was opposed by them as a threat to their labor supply. The press of 1900 noted that, "...the problem of securing boy labor is still worrying manufacturers. The truancy law, they say, is detrimental to their business" (Lynd & Lynd, 1929).

In an attempt to correct such abuses, federal and state governments have established child labor laws. Federal regulations prohibit 14- and 15-year-olds from working in nonagricultural industries: (a) during school hours; (b) before 7 A.M. or after 7 P.M., or for more than three hours a day on school days; or (c) more than 18 hours during school weeks. In addition, they may not work more than 8 hours a day or 40 hours a week during nonschool days and weeks, nor after 9 P.M. from June 1 through Labor Day. Federal laws also prohibit 14- and 15-year-olds from employment in: (a) all manufacturing and mining occupations; (b) construction, transport, public utilities, and communications occupations (with certain exceptions); and (c) a number of occupations in retail, warehousing, and food service (General Accounting Office, 1991).

State laws may also apply, and usually differ by age of the young worker. When laws differ, the stricter one takes precedence. Indiana child labor laws illustrate typical differences.

Indiana 14- and 15-year-olds are restricted to 8 hours per day, 3 hours on school days, and 40 hours per week, 23 hours during school weeks. They may not work more than 6 days per week, not before 7:00 A.M., not after 9:00 P.M., 7:00 P.M. if a school day follows.

Indiana 16-year-olds are restricted to 8-hour work days, 9 hours during the summer with written parental permission, 40 hours per week, and 48 hours during the summer. They may not work before 6:00 A.M. nor after midnight, and a maximum of 6 days a week.

Youths 17 and older can work 8 hours per day during the school year, 9 during the summer with written parental permission, 40-hour weeks, 48 if in the summer. They may not work past 11:30 P.M. on nights followed by a school day, but not on consecutive nights, and more than two school nights per week with parental permission. (Meyer, 1991)

ILLEGAL EMPLOYMENT PERSISTS

Despite laws to the contrary, literally thousands of teenagers are employed illegally today. Child labor lives on in America. Low-wage service industries find teenage workers to be ideal employees; they are willing to work dead-end jobs for minimum wages without fringe benefits, such as medical insurance or retirement plans. Working them above and beyond the limits of child labor laws is a low-profile crime not likely to be discovered or punished.

The U.S. General Accounting Office study (1991) estimated that, in 1988, about 18% of all employed 15-year-olds were working in violation of the child labor laws. Because the agency believes its procedures actually understate the percentage, it is safe to generalize that at least one 15-year-old worker in every five is probably employed in violation of federal law.

The director of the Indiana Department of Labor's Bureau of Child Labor estimated that, in 1991, one fourth of all businesses in the state that employ minors were in violation of state child labor laws (Bowman, Penn, McMullin, & VanNorman, 1991). In Florida, federal labor investigators found child labor violations in 1,460 of 3,400 businesses visited ("Children at Work," 1990). New York City labor experts estimated that as many as 10,000 children were illegally employed in the garment industry. The Labor Department's Apparel Industry Task Force does its best to police approximately 7,000 registered and illegal manufacturers with only 24 investigators (*Associated Press*, May 28, 1990).

Child labor laws are characterized by lax enforcement. One reason is the insufficient number of inspectors at both the state and national levels; it is a place to cut budgets without substantial public outcry. State agencies are also woefully understaffed; the entire state of Illinois employed only 13 child labor inspectors in 1992 (Waldman & Springen, 1992). Another reason is that this form of law enforcement is not popular with employers of teenagers, although in most cases the penalties are not severe.

Each year, thousands of violations are discovered by federal and state inspectors; if a careful and complete enforcement was to be conducted, tens of thousands of cases could be identified.

WHY WORK?

As suggested previously, Americans have deeply held beliefs that having a job promotes responsibility, strengthens character, and promotes maturity. We have a mythology of the value of working after school at the grocery store or rising before dawn to deliver newspapers in rain or snow.

Despite the purported psychological benefits that are supposed to accrue to one who works, most teenage boys enter part-time employment for money. The McDonald's corporation, one of the nation's most responsible employers of teenagers, recognizes this fact in the text of the trifold pamphlet that can be picked up at their service counter (Fig. 1).

FIGURE 1
From the text of *12 good reasons for working at McDonald's*. (1987). McDonald's corporation, OB Product No. 4008802.

1. McDonald's offers extremely flexible hours.
2. MONEY.
3. McDonald's work environment encourages friendships that last.
4. MONEY.
5. McDonald's has one of the most complete training programs around.
6. MONEY.
7. If you work at McDonald's in high school, it is easier to get a McDonald's job wherever you go after graduation.
8. MONEY.
9. McDonald's work experience leads you to greater careers.
10. MONEY.
11. Opportunities for a more permanent life-long McDonald's career exist.
12. MONEY.

The teenage boy usually takes his first part-time job for pay with personal enthusiasm and full family approval. His anticipated income is seen as being helpful in taking some of the pressure off the family budget; the costs of attending an American public school are considerable. Perhaps some contributions to the family budget will be made. It is hoped and assumed that this first job will result in increased self-confidence and independence, and will be a source of skills applicable later in the adult work world. As with many dreams these days, few of these consequences are likely to come to pass.

Evidence from almost every study is consistent: Most of the money earned by teenagers is spent on themselves (e.g., on cars and insurance; personal possessions such as fashionable clothes and CDs; and recreational activities such as movies, concert tickets, and drugs and alcohol). With few exceptions, they report little money is used to help with family expenses or is saved for college or any other future expenses.

A study of students in an Iowa high school revealed that students admitted that they worked primarily for personal consumption purposes. Some were saving for college, but only 17% of the juniors. Some helped with family finances, but only 3.3% of the seniors. The vast majority indicated that their earnings go for "clothing, records, stereos, eating out, and automobiles" (Workman, 1990).

Some of the reasoning is ironically circular. A senior recently attempted to justify a requested time extension to rewrite his late and flawed term paper. He argued that his study time was limited because he had to work extra hours to earn payments for a car that he just had to have to get to and from his job site.

Teenage workers seem to fall into this pattern, regardless of school location or size. The guidance director of a small rural high school conducted a study of her junior and senior classes, producing the results presented in Figure 2. The counselor concluded, "These students appear to be working to maintain their cars, personal appearance, and to finance their social activities" (North Hickory High School, 1991).

Figure 2
Results of a survey of the junior and senior classes of North Hickory High School, Fall 1991.

Working regularly during the school year: 35%
Working more than the legal maximum hours: 20%

Rank order of reported use of earnings:
1. dates, clothes, social expenses
2. car insurance
3. savings
4. car payments
5. saving for a car
6. saving for college

Most frequently mentioned uses of earnings:
1st: car insurance (31 mentions)
2nd: car payments (20 mentions)

The amount of money teenagers spend on themselves is quite substantial. The average employed teenager working the standard 20 hours a week at the minimum wage nets about $275 per month (Greenberger & Steinberg, 1986). In 1989, 13- to 19-year-olds spent an estimated $56 billion on themselves (Miller, 1990). They comprise an important segment of the consuming public, and their earning and spending role is often defined as essential to the economy.

Regardless of the wisdom of this spending pattern, it does establish a level of life-style that may become difficult to sustain as the teenager becomes an independent young adult. Many, if not most, teenagers who work maximum hours have more discretionary dollars to spend than they will have again for several decades. The reason is that dad is still helping with the car and insurance bills, mom is still providing meals and doing the laundry, and the rent and utilities are free. When youngsters who have established a lavish spending life-style as teenagers get out on their own in their twenties, many of them literally crash into economic realities. Maybe that explains why some parents have trouble getting the little birds to leave the nest permanently.

THE EFFECTS OF WORKING

School Grades and Test Scores
A plethora of research has proved that, after a certain point, working has negative effects upon education and grades. Data collected in California, Wisconsin, and New Hampshire show that grades begin to decline when students work more than 10 or 12 hours a week. When a student's grades begin to fall, a shrewd first question for the counselor might be, How many hours are you working?

The reasons are simple: Time spent sacking burgers, tearing ticket stubs, stocking shelves, and processing film is time not available for study and homework. Teen workers often come to school unprepared, and sometimes so tired that they doze off in class. The fact that more boys than girls work may be a clue as to why they earn lower course grades.

Facing the realities of the situation, teachers shorten reading assignments, simplify lessons, reduce out-of-class projects, and, in general, dilute the curriculum to accommodate student workers. In addition to reducing time and energy for classroom work, student workers also reduce participation in extracurricular activities. Music, drama, and even sports programs are abandoned. The combination of lower grades, lower standardized test scores, and few extraclass activities combine to weaken academic records and credentials. A lower grade-point average, a lower class rank, few extraclass activities, and lower SAT scores can result in not being accepted at the college of choice, in qualifying for scholarships, and having the background to succeed in postsecondary education. The weakened credentials can make it more difficult to get a real adult job after high school. For a teenage boy, these are distant and abstract goals. A paycheck now with his name on it is instant gratification. Unless his attention is directed specifically to future consequences, he is not likely to perceive the connection by himself.

Unintended Lessons Taught and Learned

Everybody knows the purported benefits of work. Work is said to promote responsibility and maturity, make school subjects meaningful, teach the value of money, and serve as an appropriate transition to independence and adulthood. These beliefs are deeply entrenched in the American psyche. We believe because we want to believe, not because we have much proof.

Research in this area suggests that a modification of these beliefs is now justified:

> Many of our findings will undoubtedly surprise those who advocate hefty doses of work experience for young people. Among the most striking of these findings are that extensive part-time employment may have a deleterious impact on youngsters' schooling; that working appears to promote, rather than deter, some forms of delinquent behavior; that working, especially in high-stress jobs held by many teenagers, leads to higher rates of alcohol and drug abuse; and that, for many youngsters, working fosters the development of negative attitudes toward work itself. (Greenberger & Steinberg, 1986, pp. xv–xvi)

Some of the evidence regarding what teenagers really learn at work is surprising and shocking. In their first part-time job, 62% of one large group of teens reported committing at least one of nine acts of deviance, ranging from calling in sick falsely to stealing. About 41% admitted some form of theft, and about 45% admitted some other illegal or unethical behavior (Ruggerio, Greenberger, & Steinberg, 1982).

In another study, a sample of adolescent workers were asked the following questions. The percentage of workers who said "yes" follows in parentheses (Greenberger & Steinberg, 1986, p. 144):

Did you ever give away goods or services? (29.9%)
- take things from work? (18.4%)
- put extra hours on time card? (9.4%)
- take money from work? (5.5%)
- deliberately shortchange a customer? (4.5%)
- call in sick when not? (32.3%)
- work under influence of drugs or alcohol? (16.9%)
- lied to employer to get or keep job? (6.9%)
- deliberately damage property at work? (2.0%)

The Indiana Youth Institute (Erickson, 1991) reported that only 10% of polled respondents felt that there was any relationship between their job and the careers they hoped to have as adults. Of the North Hickory High School juniors and seniors who worked regularly during the school year, 86% said that their jobs had little or no relationship to their intended future careers.

Apparently there is no reason to believe that there is a strong connection between working and the development of more mature work habits in inner-city youth. One carefully conducted study failed to find any relationship (Dale, 1987).

Do teen workers apply school concepts to the job? Job analysis has demonstrated that the average teen worker spends less than 10% of every hour using reading, writing, and arithmetic. If working at a food-service job, the proportion drops to 1 minute per hour (Greenberger & Steinberg, 1986).

The self-reliance scores of boys has been shown to actually decline significantly after taking a job (Steinberg, Greenberger, Garduque, & McAuliffe, 1982).

The jobs that teenagers typically perform are no bridge to adult careers; they are usually disconnected from any career ladder. There is little evidence that the workplaces in which most teens find jobs promote any acquisition of important skills or information. Working a great deal while in high school is often associated with higher rates of drug and alcohol abuse, cynicism about the intrinsic value of work, and self-indulgent patterns of consumption.

CHALLENGES FOR COUNSELORS

It would be as foolish for counselors to mount an all-out assault on part-time work by students as it would be for them to strive to stamp out all sexual expression. Achieving either goal is hopeless, and such attempts would only make the counselor look foolish in the process. Fortunately, there are many actions that counselors can take to ease the harsh effects of this situation.

Do not rely on evidence and statistics from sources like this book: Do some local research of your own. How many of your students are working? Doing what? For how many hours a day, a week? For what level of pay? Is there any meaningful difference in grades and participation in school activities between workers, excessive workers, and nonworkers? Do the boys who earn lower grades have their grades lowered for reasons traceable to not devoting sufficient time to their assignments? Such information is available in every school setting and is easy to collect.

Data are essential for answering some questions. For example, you may hear contentions that work does not lower grades, but that students who make lower grades work more because they find school less relevant to their lives. A comparison of the grades earned before and after they began their part-time jobs might answer this question.

Publicize your findings with administrators, teachers, students, parents, and school community. The goal is a base of reliable and valid facts from which a united stance can be constructed, accepted, and implemented.

Most schools have several quite exceptional boys who do not fit into the stereotypes. Some can work 20 hours a week, earn top grades, and be sports stars simultaneously. Every school these days seems to include several emancipated boys—youngsters who must work for basic food, shelter, and clothing expenses. This is why sweeping rules and regulations are to be discouraged in favor of guidelines, room for individual appeal and adjustments, and some understanding compassion. A professional makes judgments, rather than mindlessly enforcing rules.

Publicize federal and state employments to students, parents, teachers, and businesses in your community. Strive to eliminate the "ignorance of the law" defense.

The curriculum of the school guidance program must include the teaching of time-management skills. The failure to manage time properly is a frequent antecedent to academic disaster, at either the secondary or postsecondary levels.

It is erroneous to refer to a teenage boy "having his first job." He already has his first job: he is a worker in a knowledge and learning factory called *school*. That job usually consumes at least 7 hours a day. If he sleeps 8 hours, uses 3 hours eating and in personal grooming activities, works 2 hours, and does 2 hours of homework, he still has 2 hours for sports, cars, family, television, hobbies, girls, and loafing around with his friends. It is a tight fit. If he works more hours, it is nearly impossible.

Insist on the enforcement of child labor regulations in your school. It is ironic that some who are quick to deny driver's licenses to school dropouts, and complain that the school days and school years are too short, fall silent and look the other way when excessive and illegal employment consumes the time needed for a teenager's main job: succeeding as a student in school.

In conclusion, it is unrealistic to lobby for a state of affairs where all boys devote all of their energies to their primary job of being a student. Economic realities make it necessary for some boys to work. Social and cultural realities make it desirable for other boys to work. The key seems to be finding a reasonable balance, so that working is complementary, not competitive, to academic development. If parents, counselors, teachers, employers, and part-time workers communicate successfully, there is no reason why this balance cannot be determined for each individual boy.

REFERENCES

Associated Press. (1990, May 28). Garment industry employs kids illegally, experts say. *Terre Haute Tribune Star,* p. 1.

Bowman, S., Penn, J., McMullin, J., & VanNorman, R. (1991, May 6). Labor laws make attempt to guard kids. *The Indianapolis Star,* Children's Express, p. D8.

Children at work. (1990, March 31). *Miami Herald,* p 24A.

Coontz, S. (1992). *The way we never were.* New York: Basic Books.

Dale, M. (1987). *Economically disadvantaged students at work: Curse or blessing.* Unpublished doctoral dissertation, Ohio State University, Columbus, OH.

Erickson, J. B. (1991). *Indiana youth poll: Youth's views of life beyond high school. F.Y.I.* Indianapolis, IN: The Indiana Youth Institute.

General Accounting Office. (1991, June). *Child labor: Characteristics of working children* (Report No. GAO/HRD-91-83BR). Briefing report presented to Congressional Requesters,

Greenberger, E., & Steinberg, L. (1986). *When teenagers work.* New York: Basic Books.

Hoyt, K. B., Evans, R. N., Mockin, E. F., & Mangum, G. L. (1972). *Career education: What it is and how to do it.* Salt Lake City, UT: Olympus.

Lynd, R. S., & Lynd, H. M. (1929). *Middletown.* New York: Harcourt Brace.

Mason, P. P. (1976, January 17). Working in America: To many, jobs are a big bore, at any salary. *The National Observer.* p. B3.

Meyer, K. (1991, May 6). Labor laws make attempt to guard kids. *Indianapolis Star,* p. D8.

Miller, A. (1990). Work and what it's worth. *Newsweek Special Edition, The New Teens.*

North Hickory High School. (1991). *A survey of the junior and senior classes.* Unpublished field research project report, Indiana State University, Terre Haute, IN.

Ruggerio, M., Greenberger, E., & Steinberg, L. (1982). Occupational deviance among first-time workers. *Youth and Society, 13,* 423–448.

Steinberg, L., Greenberger, E., Garduque, L., & McAuliffe, S. (1982). High-school students in the labor force: Some costs and benefits to schooling and learning. *Educational Evaluation and Policy Analysis, 4,* 363–372.

Trends. (1993, February). All work and no play. *NEA Today,* p. 6.

U. S. Department of Education. (1991). *A profile of the American 8th grader.* Washington, DC: U.S. Government Printing Office.

Waldman, S., & Springen, K. (1992, November 16). Too old, too fast? *Newsweek,* pp. 80, 82–84, 88.

Workman, B. (1990, April). The teenager and the world of work: Alienation at West High? *Phi Delta Kappan,* pp. 628–631.

CHAPTER 8

CAREER AND LIFE PLANNING

In the mid-1990s, the United States is in the midst of profound social, economic, and political changes. No citizen, regardless of sex, age, or ethnic background, will escape the consequences. The role of work is one aspect of American life that is undergoing trans-formation: from what it has been to who knows what. Planning one's life and career and converting it to reality has never been easy, but at least up to now the choices were predictable and the targets remained still.

In previous generations, changes were gradual and evolutionary, not sudden and revolutionary. Now it is like trying to participate in a sport and having your efforts interrupted frequently by abrupt and fundamental changes in the rules. Consequently, although many boys today are successfully mastering the new life- and career-planning process, too many others are not.

THE IMPORTANCE OF CHOICE AND DEVELOPMENT

The outcomes of individual career- and life-planning decisions de-termine the nature of the nation's labor force and the quality of life of its citizens.

What Is Good and Bad for the Economy
Business, industry, and government would rejoice if there were a perfect match between supply and demand of all levels of workers. In the United States, we do not formally sort, screen, and direct individuals to irreversible career tracks. Americans choose their careers, and not all choose as "wisely" as their elders would prefer. The temptation is to step in and make decisions *for* individuals, not *with* them—for the good of the nation and economy, of course.

What Is Good and Bad for the Individual

For the individual, work in our culture is a structure around which a complete life-style is developed. Many find their identities and self-concepts through what they do for a living. The life-style one can afford comes from the income from occupational activities. The job is the nucleus around which life grows. Observe what is happening today to those who suddenly find themselves unemployed. If to *be* somebody you have to *do* something, what happens if you cannot find a legitimate setting in which to perform? One solution is to seek a role on the margins of society, as noted in chapter 6 on criminal gangs.

Sometimes these two values are in harmony: society wants more engineers, engineering is perceived as a macho way of life that leads to material success, the preparation system limits access and screens out all but the best, and everybody wins.

Sometimes these forces are not in harmony: Society wants more nurses, teachers, and social workers, but does not place the economic resources and reinforcements in place. Everybody loses.

Pressures are exerted on the schools and counselors from two directions. The economic and postsecondary interests want the schools to sort, screen, and stream students into vocational paths that provide business and industry with exactly the desired number of workers who are ready to make them a profit the first day on the job. From another direction comes the voices that contend that our primary loyalty should be the welfare of the individual student, even when that is contrary to what seems at the time not to match the immediate needs of the economic system.

In some cases, the individual can have it both ways. In others, a dilemma forces a choice between what is best for the nation's economy and what is best for him as an individual human being.

Another chorus of confusing and contradictory messages assault adolescent eardrums, this time with competing visions of what the work world is going to be like in the years just ahead.

From one direction comes predictions of a wonder world of technology that lies just over the horizon, with computers, robots, lasers, miracle drugs, and miracle machines—a Buck Rogers, Star-Wars world. A rosy picture is painted of exotic occupations requiring high levels of mathematics and science abilities, a shorter work week, and higher pay.

At the same time, there are dire predictions of economic and social disintegration, fewer jobs, lower wages, periods of long-term unemployment for almost everybody, by-passed minority groups, career interruption and uncertainty, and a permanent two-class social system (McDaniels, 1989). Sudden displacement of workers is not a new phenomenon; it has been going on since knitting machines were installed in British textile mills. The famous "pony express" lasted only 5 days after the first telegraph message was sent. The difference today is that the losses are structural, permanent, and involve highly educated and skilled workers.

Caught in the crossfire of current political, social, and economic pronouncements, it is no wonder that so many boys are bewildered and confused. Which messages and which messengers should be trusted? The babble can be overwhelming and can trigger aberrant responses.

THE CAREER- AND LIFE-PLANNING PROBLEMS OF BOYS

Most of what we understand about the career- and life-planning status and development of adolescent boys presents a mixture of stress, indecision, nonchalance, and immaturity.

Dysfunctional Reactions

Once upon a time, it was relatively easy for young men to move from school to a job, and develop that job into a career. That fairy tale is over. Young men in today's job and career market face forces that create anxiety, uncertainty, and stress.

Counselors talk about "career ladders," but in recent years many of the lower rung jobs have been removed and exported to foreign countries. High school graduates have great difficulty in finding nonminimum-wage jobs. All around them they see parents and older brothers losing their jobs for reasons not associated with their performance as good workers.

Postsecondary schooling is expensive, and even then there is no guarantee of a job after graduation, with income (i.e., loans) to repay. It is depressing for many potential students to learn that, at 8% interest, a college loan of $24,750 must be paid back by payments of $300.29 every month for 10 years. Because the bank suggests that graduates should provide 8% of their income toward their college loan, this would require a job that pays $45,044 (Bank of America, 1991). Boys who do not take this gamble are not unrealistic.

It is no wonder that, for many boys, thinking about their future occupational role is an uncomfortable topic to be avoided—like thinking about their eventual death. Several unsuccessful patterns of coping with such stresses have been identified.

Some boys become passive; their bodies may be in school, but their minds are elsewhere. Not necessarily troublemakers, they give only sporadic or token attention to classroom tasks and assignments. They perceive no relationship between what they are asked to learn in school and how it will be of personal benefit in their world as they know it. Many become chronic truants, later to drop out of school ill-prepared to function adequately in either the economic or the social systems of society. Some boys reject long-term potential benefits for short-term gratifications. Alcohol and drugs are pain killers, and offer at least temporary escape from their intolerable situation.

The role of provider and consumer is embedded in many definitions of *masculinity*. No job = no money = no things. The male has been seen as the hunter, the provider, and the source of economic resources for the family. As explained in chapter 6, if boys cannot acquire status, security, power, and money by working at a job, they may seek it outside society's approved establishments.

The Career Pattern Study
For 21 years, Donald Super and his team of researchers followed the career development of 103 boys in an upstate New York community. This classic longitudinal study's findings produced major contributions to our understanding of the career- and life-planning process among boys (Super et al., 1957).

The first data were collected when the boys were just beginning high school, and the last were collected when they were approximately 36 years old. Comparing project findings from the 9th and 12th grades is especially relevant (Jordaan, Heyde, Bennett, & Super, 1979):

1. Vocational preferences that were expressed by the high school seniors were not more appropriate or realistic than the ones they expressed when they were high school freshmen.
2. Their career development did not seem to proceed in the direction of more realistic, more appropriate choices. Preferences tended to be "unstable, uncertain, and unrealistic." Only one half of the seniors were considering choices in line with their measured interests and abilities, knew very much about the

occupation they said they might enter, or knew what they would have to do to qualify.

3. At both levels, the use of appropriate sources of information, knowledge of the work world, and plans for achieving their goals were "unimpressive if not seriously deficient." Most knew "relatively little" about their announced career preference.

4. Two thirds of the seniors had little or no confidence in their career goals, and had done nothing to implement their preferences.

In commenting on the situation, the authors stated:

> In working with high school youth, two questions are fundamental: How ready are they to make the decisions that parents, teachers, and society expect or require of them? If they are not ready, and these decisions—for administrative or other reasons—cannot be postponed, what can be done to help them develop the necessary degree of readiness?" (Jordaan et al., 1979, p. 196)

Because this study was completed in the mid-1970s, it is possible that our career- and life-planning guidance has become more effective. No convincing evidence that the situation has improved significantly has yet surfaced, and we still do not have satisfactory answers to the questions asked previously.

The Indiana State University Studies

Over a 3-year period, researchers from the Indiana State University Department of Counseling worked with 71 Indiana junior high and middle schools in a comprehensive equity career-guidance project. Activities were orchestrated, and data were collected several times from 6,756 boys and girls in Grades 6, 7, and 8 (Boyer & Jessell, 1988; Jessell & Boyer, 1989).

The project put forth the following model as an ideal status of career and life planning for a junior high/middle school student:

1. I have given some thought to my future career and the kind of life I would like to have for myself when I become an adult.

2. As of today, I have several possibilities on my list.

3. Among those possibilities are one or two probabilities.

4. However, if something more interesting, attractive, and desirable comes to my attention, I am willing to give it serious consideration and may change my mind.

One part of the investigation involved 857 students in several project schools. It was discovered that the young adolescents who had a wide range of realistic career attitudes and perceived abilities, who felt that a wide variety of careers were personally possible, and who would consider many of them as a career were more likely to: (a) have a positive sense of personal worth and self-esteem, (b) feel able to use personal and occupational information, (c) be female, and (d) come from a middle-class, two-parent family.

When data from all of the project substudies were summarized, a consistent pattern emerged: junior high/middle school boys were succeeding less often and less well in facing and mastering the career- and life-planning process (Beymer, 1989).

PRACTICAL APPLICATIONS OF THEORETICAL INSIGHTS

Vocational guidance began in the first decade of this century when a visionary YMCA director first worked with boys off the streets of Boston. Parsons (1909) left us with the first written set of recommendations on how to be helpful. From those humble beginnings, several bright and creative minds have provided us with at least partial insights on this process.

Americans are practical people who are not likely to instinctively recognize that there is nothing as practical as a good theory. Theories may not give us final answers, but they are invaluable in helping us ask the appropriate questions and suggesting when and how to provide timely guidance and counseling services.

Ginzberg (1952) was the first to point out that career choice is not an event, but an ongoing process. For some time it was assumed that, like Saul, individuals sooner or later would come upon their own "burning bush," and that sudden insight would settle the matter once and for all. Divine revelation of one's best and most appropriate career path would be efficient, but that is not the way it really happens. Ginzberg started the developmental point of view, which holds that, in reality, career development is a life-long process characterized by stages that unfold in a systematic order, and that compromise is an essential component of every choice and decision.

Super (1957) incorporated and expanded this concept into his comprehensive theory, and, through research, demonstrated the age-linked, progressive, hierarchical, cumulative, and predictable sequence. Counselors who are insightful and informed on the typical problems of the age group they serve are much better able to provide appropriate assistance.

Super also helped us understand that individuals are less inter-ested in finding something to *do* than they are in finding some-thing to *be*. He is responsible for much of our understanding of the importance of the self-concept in choice and job satisfaction, life stages, and role conflicts.

Holland (1973) provided us with a simple and highly useful sys-tem of categorizing people and occupations. Research on his sys-tem has been so impressive that the Holland codes have been in-corporated into many other approaches and assessment devices (Bruch, 1978). One of his major contributions is his insistence that we find ways to help our clients help themselves and find satisfac-tory answers to their concerns, rather than depending on a counse-lor to tell them. As a result, the counselor who wants to develop a comprehensive career- and life-planning curriculum can find a large number of printed and electronic resources based on the Holland system.

Krumboltz (1983) demonstrated that what one believes about self, world, and opportunities predicts the actions that will and will not occur. His social-learning model emphasizes the important role of environmental conditions and events, as well as the instrumental and observational learning that occurs away from the school as well as in the classroom (Krumboltz, Mitchell, & Jones, 1979).

CHALLENGES FOR COUNSELORS

Resist and Release Some of the Pressures

Young boys are targets of pressure from parents, the press, teachers, and counselors to make early and final career choices, usually from a listing that the latter groups find to be in their best interest. If and when the pressure to make decisions becomes excessive, young males can ease their anxieties by making a hasty, uninformed choice and publicly announcing it. This process has been titled "premature closure" (Beymer, 1989). It is premature because it occurs in ad-vance of the knowledge and understandings of alternatives, of the consequences of the stated choice, or both. It is closure because the temporary, counterfeit decision blocks him from considering other options during those years he clutches it like a security blanket. This phenomenon has been identified more often among boys.

Many significant others in the boy's life want him to be an early decider. School principals want to know how many class sections to schedule. Parents want to have assurance that their children are moving toward economic independence and career satisfaction. Adolescent boys feel increasingly inadequate as they fail to see a definite career path from where they are to where they want to go. It would be helpful to "back off" from well-meaning attempts to force choices before the chooser is equipped and ready to make them.

One of counselors' first goals for career and life planning is to make the world safe for thoughtful uncertainty—a mark of intelligence, not failure, in times like these. Boys need to know that nobody can see 10 years into the future, and that decisions follow the model of successive shaping, not divine revelation.

Give All Boys a Fair Share of Attention and Services

Most schools find the time and resources to minister to the needs of the top 25% and the bottom 25% of the student body. Community pressures encourage the former; laws mandate the latter. Those in between these extreme groups have been called "the forgotten half."

> Half of our high school students finish schooling knowing that we as taxpayers and private contributors will give them an added chance to further their education and sharpen their skills. The American people have created, and subsidize in a variety of ways, some 3,500 public and private postsecondary educational institutions—all designed to provide continuing opportunity for personal and career development....
>
> But for the other half, especially the students who did not fare as well in school, we do little, and we seem untroubled by our omission. When these young people leave high school, with or without a diploma, they are on their own. (William T. Grant Foundation Commission on Work, Family, and Citizenship, 1988, p. 59)

Adelman (1993) surveyed the situation and concluded that the "forgotten half" is a little less than half and at least two-thirds male.

The College Board conducted a coast-to-coast study of guidance services in American high schools (Interim Report, 1986). The board reported that "The typical [counselor] day described is divided between responding to students in crisis and performing the numerous clerical and accounting functions associated with scheduling, attendance, discipline, testing, and college applications" (p. 15). It also reported that "assistance from a counselor increased with the socioeconomic status of the student, and was greatest for students in the academic curriculum" (p. 10).

In its *Final Report* (1986), the board confirmed that "counselor time is divided between students who are in trouble in school or in their personal lives, and the students who are assertively pursuing postsecondary school opportunities...counselors are concerned that they are "losing the kids in the middle..." (p. 41). Another conclusion was especially critical: "Those who need most help get least in schools" (p. 3).

Apparently there is nothing we will not do, and no service we will not provide, for the college-bound student. In many schools, the guidance program is evaluated on the basis of how many seniors announce their intentions to enroll in some college or university, and how many dollars in scholarships, grants, and awards have been harvested by the elite of the senior class. Attending to the needs and demands of this segment of the school population is a matter of highest priority in most schools. We have been so preoccupied with those who go to college that we have almost ignored those who do not.

Society and taxpayers are extremely generous to assisting high school graduates make the transition to college. How much does it cost to recruit one college freshman? One recent cable television financial network estimated the cost to be $2,500. That sum accounts for such expenses as admissions personnel, school counselor time for applications and letters of recommendation, travel, videotapes, brochures, catalogs, campus visits, postage, telephone calls, and secretarial services.

In its investigation of the "forgotten half," the William T. Grant Foundation (1988) estimated that each student enrolled in an institution of higher education is the beneficiary of a public and private subsidy of about $5,000 per academic year for each of 4 or more years. This figure, which includes scholarships and grants, subsidized and guaranteed loans, free or subsidized college tuition, and other forms of public and private aid, often tops $20,000. The study concluded that, "Youth not going on to college are starved for support" (p. 4).

At the same time, society is not generous or supportive toward the student who attempts a successful transition from high school to the workplace. A letter or two of recommendation and the graduate launches into the unknown on his own. The situation is unjust and needs to be brought into balance.

All of this is ironic indeed because *going* to college is not at all synonymous with *graduating* from college. An Educational Testing

Service (ETS) report states that only half of the top high school seniors get college degrees within 7 years of high school graduation (Dodge, 1991).

Adjustments are long overdue, and several alternatives have been suggested.

1. Guidance staffs could budget 25% of their time to failing students, special-education students, and extremely troublesome students; 25% to the academically bright and college-bound; and 50% for those in between.

2. The William T. Grant Foundation suggests three ways in which the needs of the forgotten half can be met: (a) commit the resources required to pay for enough counselors to meet the needs of all students; (b) redefine the role of teachers to restore them to meaningful participation in the guidance program through home-based or family groupings; and (c) abandon the idea of counselors within schools, and shift responsibilities to neighborhood social service centers and labor offices.

3. Another way would be to structure the use of allocated time and resources to ensure that more students get the attention and services they need and deserve. Gysbers and colleagues (Gysbers, 1990; Gysbers, Hughey, Starr, & Lapan, 1992) recently put forth a sound and flexible model for allocating scarce guidance and counseling time between alternative needs and populations. This "Missouri Model" separates the work of the school counselor into four categories:

    a) The Guidance Curriculum: classroom presentations, units, videotapes, outside consultants, group activities, special events/days;

    b) Individual Planning: testing, assessment, and appraisal; advisement, placement, educational, and vocational planning;

    c) Responsive Services: individual counseling, group counseling, crisis counseling, referral, consultation with teachers and parents; and

    d) System Support: record keeping, research and development, staff/community public relations, professional development, committees and advisory boards, community outreach, program planning/management and operations.

To ensure a fair distribution of professional attention to all categories, the guidance staff budgets percentages of time to be allocated to each category. Percentages can differ somewhat by grade level, as illustrated in Table 3. The development and implementation of this model will likely result in a reduction in time currently devoted to some categories, but that is compensated by guaranteed attention to other functions and students just as worthy of attention and services.

TABLE 3
Percentages of time allocation to the four functions as suggested by 65 junior high/middle schools and high schools that field-tested the model of Gysbers et al. (1990).

Functions	JHS/MS	HS
Guidance Curriculum	25-35%	15-20%
Individual Planning	15-25%	25-35%
Responsive Services	30-40%	25-35%
System Support	10-15%	15-25%
Total	100%	100%

4. If school counselors are to continue to serve as recruiting officers for colleges and universities, then whenever a student is accepted, a fee should be paid to the school in recognition of professional and clerical services provided. Such funds could support a counselor to work with seniors who do not elect to continue their education.

This fund could be augmented by establishing some fair, but modest cost for excessive services. In one midwestern high school, a bright senior applied to 25 medical schools, tying up the office staff for 2 weeks. Perhaps each graduate should be entitled to two or three free applications, and pay a reasonable fee for the rest.

If these aggressive alternatives seem unreasonable and unfair, they should be compared with the existing state of affairs, which is definitely unreasonable and unfair. We live in a time of frequent calls for "justice" and "equity." Some we cannot ease; for those that we can, we should.

Provide Appropriate Services to Those Who Are Late Deciders

About February 1st of each year, high school counselors tend to swing their attention to the junior class. By that date, the college applications, letters of recommendation, and financial-aid forms are in the mail. If some senior, or graduate, decides late in the year or during the summer that postsecondary education of some type would be in his or her best interest, who is around to help?

Perhaps the traditional office hours for guidance services (i.e., during daytime school hours) need to be revised. Guidance services might be provided at times and in places that are more convenient to busy work and family schedules. This might mean moving out of the school to community locations, and having late afternoon and evening office hours.

Lend Your Support to Broadening the School Curriculum

One of our biggest problems today is that many students fail to find meaning in the mandated curriculum that is prejudiced toward the vocational preparation of future workers in academic factories called *colleges*. Students not oriented in this direction have legitimate questions about what they are learning and where such learning can lead.

One of contemporary society's great myths is that business and industry want entry-level employees who have high levels of specific vocational skills. In fact, what employers value is a young worker with a cluster of good work attitudes and habits: (a) the ability to function without close supervision, (b) respect for others, and (c) a positive view of authority (Erdman, 1992).

Similar findings emerged from a Johns Hopkins University survey of 4,080 company personnel officers responsible for hiring high school graduates (Crain, 1984). The officers were asked what traits were considered most important in high school graduates. The ranking and frequency percent mentioned are as follows.

1. (94%) "Dependability—coming to work regularly and on time."
2. (82%) "Able to accept supervision; proper attitudes about work and supervisors."
3. (74%) "Able to get along well with people."
4. (65%) "Able to read materials about as difficult as a daily newspaper."
5. (56%) "Able to perform basic arithmetic."

The employing officials reported that a strong personal impression in the interview was important, in addition to good recommendations from a manager who knows the applicant, strong recommendations from previous employers, and good character references. Only 18% of the hiring officials reported that a high score on a written test was very important in their decision. Only 12% placed high value on school grades.

A labor department consultant reported similar findings:

> Executives at the companies we studied weren't bitching about skills.... They said, "We'll train workers if the schools can produce them with the right attitudes." Indeed, good grades in school are a poor predictor of job success. AT&T, renowned for sophisticated hiring techniques, has found extracurricular activities a better gauge. (Erdman, 1992, p. 18)

Before becoming secretary of labor in the Clinton administration, Robert Reish listed four clusters of skills and abilities he contended were crucial to the work force of the near future (Reish, 1991). He called these "skills of symbolic analysis."

1. Abstraction: the capacity to order and make meaning of a massive flow of information by shaping raw data into workable patterns.
2. System Thinking: the capacity to see the parts in relation to the whole, and to see why problems arise.
3. Experimental Inquiry: the capacity to set up procedures to test and evaluate alternative ideas.
4. Collaboration: the capacity to engage in active communication and dialogue to get a variety of perspectives and to create consensus when that is necessary.

Schools today seem to assume that there is only one path to a sound and functional education—a specific sequence of specific classes. In fact, there are many routes, and we need to identify even more. Counselors can help.

The National Occupational Information Coordinating Committee (NOICC; 1989) published a comprehensive series of guidelines to guide, support, and strengthen career- and life-planning activities. Versions are available for elementary, junior high/middle, and high schools, and suggest competencies and outcome indicators that can be used in tracking progress. These materials are a valuable resource for schools either in the process of strengthening an existing program or launching new ventures.

Many new curriculum-reform models lie just ahead, such as Tech-Prep, Workforce Development, and others. Many have the potential of providing experiences that will result in more boys remaining connected to the learning system longer. Many of these thrusts give local schools wide latitude in definition, structure, and operation. Counselors need to be involved in any and all reform movements that have the potential to offer better learning opportunities for students.

Counselors Who do Must Stop "Putting Down" Vocational Education

Too many counselors and other educators cling to the belief that vocational education is little more than narrow minimum-skills training for academically marginal students—preparation for manual, low-pay, low-status work. Vocational education is not auto body shop anymore; it is illogical and unreasonable to categorize electronics as a nonacademic subject.

In the recent past, workers sold their muscle energy, and manipulated things and materials. The next generation of workers will sell their mental energy, and manipulate abstractions such as data and information. Many of them will earn more money and have more job security than many college graduates. We are easing into an era where the majority of all good jobs will involve "thinking for a living" (Marshall & Tucker, 1992). What used to be called *vocational education* is becoming an important entry path to these emerging careers. It is bad enough to be labeled, patronized, harassed, and ridiculed by peers because you are a vocational-education student; it is intolerable to suffer such abuse from the faculty.

Conduct Annual Follow-up Studies

Facts about your students' fate after they leave your school are invaluable in illustrating what kind of lives are lived by graduates. Such investigations need not be expensive nor difficult.

One "quick and dirty" method is to take last year's school yearbook down to the school cafeteria and have students tell you where the seniors of last year are. When two different students independently tell you the same thing, accept it as a fact. A few telephone calls can clear up most of the straggler cases. This method is likely to produce information on a higher percent of the class than mailed questionnaires, and it is quicker and cheaper.

Do it for the past two graduating classes to illustrate the difference between "going to college" and staying there, and the kind of entry-level jobs that await those who do not obtain postsecondary education.

Reconsider Old Myths and Motivators
It has been trendy and fashionable to stress the work role as the best way to attain personal life success, identity, and expression. Reality demonstrates that all jobs are routine and boring some of the time, and some all of the time. New workers may have to find satisfactions before, between, and after work. There is danger in teaching "you are what you do"; if and when you are told you are no longer needed to do anything, there is a danger of feeling that you are nothing.

Minority Blues
We know so little about if and how minority males differ in their needs and learning styles (Lee, 1992). We do know that there are many times more African-American dentists than African-American professional athletes, but apparently this is a secret to most minority males. Theorists should give us more insights on how to meet the unique needs of boys of color, and provide us with assessment devices we can afford on restricted budgets. We continue to operate on the assumption that all boys today have career choices, yet not even all middle-class White boys have this luxury today. Counselors pontificate about "choosing a career"; most boys would be happy to find a job at all.

Counselors Alone Cannot Get the Job Done
We do not have, nor are we ever likely to have, a sufficient number of school counselors to provide each and every student with personalized, individualized career guidance. Other educators and electronic media can make major contributions, and these are invaluable allies.

A few decades ago, "teacher counselors" were numerous, and teacher sponsors of home rooms performed many guidance functions. As full-time counselors joined the faculty to do more, teachers did less until, in many schools, it became traditional for them to do little or nothing in the form of group guidance activities.

This trend is reversing with the advent of a concept called "teacher advisor programs." Myrick and Myrick (1990) presented many examples of how classroom teachers can be brought back into the guidance program, with benefits to students and teachers.

The desktop microcomputer and the video recorder provide technological opportunities for lifting a great portion of the burden off career counselors. Comprehensive systems like Discover, SIGI, and COIN can lead the boy through a complete spectrum of planning activities. Many shorter microcomputer programs perform brilliantly in dealing with single topics. Like it or not, many adolescents have learned to learn by watching a television screen, not by reading pamphlets. Many commercial sources provide catalogs of tapes covering a gamut of topics. If the budget is insufficient, community organizations and individuals can be contacted and invited to make contributions to the guidance department's electronic library.

Ask Answerable Questions

Most young males find it difficult to answer the question, What are you going to do after you graduate from school? Remember that when you ask a junior high school boy to tell you what he expects to do when his formal education is behind him, you are asking him to look farther into the future than he can remember in his past. The 13-year-old will be 23 when he graduates from college. Few adults know what they will be doing when they are 75% older than they are today. It is no wonder that boys are tongue-tied when the counselor or their Aunt Opal asks this question.

A much better question—one that can be answered—is, What kind of a life do you want for yourself when your formal education has been completed? Once an answer to that inquiry is developed and discussed, the subnect can be returned to the present. Another good question is, What abilities, interests, talents, and skills do you have that can be developed in the next few years of free school so that you can have your desired life-style?

High school is a $20,000 scholarship, and after that the boy will pay retail. If he can perceive the relationship between what he can learn in school to the kinds of career choices he can make to obtain the life-style he wants as a young man, education can become more satisfying for both those who deliver it and those who receive it. Career and life planning is all too often perceived, even by counselors, as a peripheral activity. The facts are that it has the potential to help students assume increased responsibility for their own education and lives.

When doing career- and life-planning counseling with boys, remember that it is primarily a cluster of decisions about how he wants to live his life, which includes how to earn a living. It will be easier to come up with satisfactory answers if the issues are considered in this order.

In summary, young people today are entering a period of history characterized by the necessity to make a lifelong series of decisions relating to the role of work in their lives. Everybody wins if they learn in school the nature of this game and the skills and strategies that will help them to play it successfully.

REFERENCES

Adelman, C. (1993, September 10). The changing "forgotten half": It's less than half and two-thirds male. *Education Week, 7*, 41, 56.

Bank of America. (1991). *Repaying your student loan.* BankAmerica Corporation, Los Angeles, CA.

Beymer, L. (1989). *Improving equity career guidance in Indiana junior high and middle schools: Results and recommendations from a three year pronect* (Equity Career Guidance Monograph #4). Terre Haute, IN: Indiana State University Department of Counseling. (ERIC Document Reproduction Service No. ED 311 340)

Boyer, M., & Jessell, J. (1988). *Career expectations of Indiana's young adolescents* (Equity Career Guidance Pronect Monograph #1). Terre Haute, IN: Indiana State University Department of Counseling.

Bruch, M. A. (1978). Holland's topology applied to client-counselor interaction: Implications for counseling with men. *Counseling Psychologist, 7*(4) 26–32.

Crain, R. L. (1984). *The quality of American high school graduates: What personnel officers say and do about it* (Tech. Rep. No. 354). Baltimore, MD: Johns Hopkins University, Center for Social Organization of Schools.

Dodge, S. (1991, June 5). Study finds only half of top high-school seniors get college degrees within 7 years of graduation. *The Chronicle of Higher Education*, p. 1.

Erdman, A. (1992, August). What's wrong with workers. *Fortune, 136*(3), 18.

Final Report, Keeping the options open: Recommendations. (1986). New York: Commission on Precollege Guidance and Counseling, College Entrance Examination Board.

Ginzberg, E. (1952). Toward a theory of occupational choice. *Occupations, 30*, 491–494.

Gysbers, N. C. (1990). *Comprehensive guidance programs that work.* Ann Arbor, MI: ERIC Counseling and Personnel Services Clearinghouse.

Gysbers, N. C., Hughey, K. F., Starr, M., & Lapan, R. T. (1992). Improving school guidance programs: A framework for program, personnel, and results evaluation. *Journal of Counseling and Development, 70,* 565–570.

Holland, J. L. (1973). *Making vocational choices: A theory of vocational personalities and work environments.* Englewood Cliffs, NJ: Prentice-Hall.

Interim Report, Keeping the options open: An overview. (1986). New York: Commission on Precollege Guidance and Counseling, College Entrance Examination Board.

Jessell, J., & Boyer, M. (1989). *Career expectations among Indiana junior high and middle school students: A second survey* (Equity Career Guidance Monograph #3). Terre Haute, IN: Indiana State University Department of Counseling.

Jordaan, J. P., Heyde, M. B., & Super, D. E. (1979). *Vocational maturity during the high school years.* New York: Teachers College Press.

Krumboltz, J. H., Mitchell, A. M., & Jones, G. B. (1979). *Social learning and career decision making.* Cranston, RI: The Carroll Press.

Krumboltz, J. D. (1983). *Private rules in career decision making.* Columbus, OH: National Center for Research in Vocational Education.

Lee, C. C. (1992). *Empowering young black males.* Ann Arbor, MI: ERIC Counseling and Personnel Services Clearinghouse.

Marshall, R., & Tucker, M. (1992). *Thinking for a living: Education and the wealth of nations.* New York: Basic Books.

McDaniels, C. (1989). *The changing workplace: Career counseling strategies for the 1990's and beyond.* San Francisco: Jossey-Bass.

Myrick, R. D., & Myrick, L. S. (1990). *The teacher advisor program: An innovative approach to school guidance.* Ann Arbor, MI: ERIC Counseling and Personnel Services Clearinghouse.

National Occupational Information Coordinating Committee. (1989). *National career development guidelines.* Washington, DC: Author.

Parsons, F. (1909). *Choosing a vocation.* Garrett Park, MD: Garrett Park Press.

Reish, R. (1991). *The work of nations: Preparing ourselves for 21st century capitalism.* New York: Random House.

Super, D. E. (1957). *The psychology of careers.* New York: Harper.

Super, D. E., Crites, J. O., Hummel, R. C., Moser, H. P., Overstreet, P. L., & Warnath, C. F. (1957). *Vocational development: A framework for research.* New York: Columbia University Press.

William T. Grant Foundation Commission on Work, Family, and Citizenship. (1988). *The forgotten half: Non-college youth in America.* Washington, DC: Author.

CHAPTER 9

MAKING A
MEANINGFUL DIFFERENCE

The first eight chapters of this book focused on aspects of the lives of young boys today, and highlighted the obstacles they face in developing from little boys to men. Some of the issues seem beyond remediation by anything any one person can do. Be not discouraged: You can make a meaningful difference.

The central core of counselor education is the development of skills: giving attention, listening, and being empathetic. These are powerful therapeutic techniques that should not be underestimated. Many youngsters today have little experience with an adult who will listen and understand. Just giving boys some attention and acknowledging that you understand what they are experiencing can be very helpful. If and when the boy client begins to say to himself, "I am in the safe, nonjudgmental presence of a person who is actually listening to what I have to say and understands my point of view," change has already begun. One hint of the efficacy of attention may be found in analysis of student athletes' grades. One would expect that, during the sports season, athletes' grades would decline because time spent in practice and playing detracts from study time. However, many counselors report that student athletes' grades often decline *after* the season closes when there is more time for academic activities. Having to stay academically eligible is a strong motivator. Another explanation is that, during the sports season, both teachers and peers give student athletes a lot of attention and support that drifts away when the team completes the season. Perhaps boys perform up to our expectations, and perhaps our expectations are not always challenging.

This phenomenon resembles the placebo effect in medicine. For years it has been known that ineffective drugs and therapies can cure if patients sincerely believe in them. Some of the evidence is astonishing. Research at the National Institute of Arthritis found that *anything* done to an arthritis patient, if the patient believes in it, will result in a response approaching a 20%–30% decrease in inflammation. The simple fact of receiving treatment, or perhaps even getting on a waiting list to receive treatment, has banished symptoms of migraine headaches, peptic ulcers, chronic pain, and swelling of joints (Orlock, 1993). Some research at Northwestern University, based on a sample of 3,000 clients, discovered that 20% of subjects experienced noticeable symptom relief by the mere act of making an appointment with a therapist, even when it was later canceled.

Much remains to be learned about the mind–body connection, but one principle has been established: Beliefs can alter body chemistry, attitudes, and behavior. If the counselor takes the time to show genuine interest and concern, almost anything is possible.

Do not disparage small changes. Remember that a change in course direction of only a few degrees can result in your Boston plane landing in Seattle rather than San Francisco. Sometimes it takes time to see the visible outcomes of guidance and counseling interventions.

One person cannot do everything—but one person can do something, and can multiply those efforts by enlisting others to the cause. When helping adults provide nurturing environments for boys, the challenge is to find ways to tell them what they *need* to hear even when it is not *what* they may want to hear, and in such a manner that they reject neither the message nor the messenger.

Providing appropriate and timely developmental and remedial services to boys is a sobering challenge for counselors. If we do not accept it, who will?

REFERENCES

Orlock, C. (1993). The case of the perplexing prescription. *Arthritis Today, 7* (2), 28–32.